MW00414812

A Chateau in Provence

CHARLEY WOOD

EUROPEAN EXPERIENCES PUBLISHING

A Chateau in Provence

First published in 2011 in the USA by European Experiences Publishing.

ISBN   9781461171119

www.european-experiences.com

www.luberonexperience.com

2011

A Chateau in Provence

www.charleywoodbooks.com

Chapter One

Sam Baker had looked forward to this moment since dawn - ten hours and fifteen miles ago. That's when he had given in to the persistent nagging of his alarm clock and with Herculean effort coaxed his still aching feet from the warm bed and stuffed them back into his soaked hiking boots.

Yesterday's sudden summer downpour had been Mother Nature's farewell reminder of her fickleness. He shivered at the thought, but at least now it was finally over. Two weeks on the trail and now all he wanted was a comfortable chair to drop his weary body into, a place to rest his aching feet, and someone to bring him a cold drink.

Preferably, an ice cold beer.

Sam got his wish, that place to rest his tired body and sore feet, and a beer so cold that the most jaded Bavarian would have smiled in appreciation.

Of course, he would later ask himself many times if that

beer could possibly be worth the price he would end up paying.

For Sam, the day had started routinely enough . . . . like each day of the previous two weeks. His wife Diane, daughter Beth, and he had just finished a long distance hike through the Luberon region of Provence in southern France. They would wake early each morning, eat a breakfast that would power a stonemason for the day and hit the trail.

The trail, a *Grande Randonnée*, was part of an extensive system of trails that abounded in Provence, crisscrossing the countryside and providing the perfect way to see the country close up.   After hours of exploring ruined castles and ancient forts, walking past miles of vineyards, olive groves, lavender fields and taking pictures by the hundreds, the Bakers   would finish each day in much the same way -a hot shower, a multi-course dinner, in bed by dusk, asleep in seconds.

This fourteenth and final day found the American family, hot and weary, climbing the last few kilometers up a narrow, twisting road to a perched village near the market town of Apt.

This part of Provence, the Luberon, was peppered with dozens of these small villages, some clinging to the sides of hills, others crowning rocky promontories, all looking as if a gentle nudge could send them sliding into the valley below - an avalanche of medieval village. But with several hundred years history behind them, they proved to be well anchored to their foundations; built from stone gouged and formed from the very mountains on which they rested; the ancient rift between stone and mountain now healed by the passing of centuries.

It occurred to Sam that the medieval builders of these *villages perché* were military geniuses. Sam, himself, was a building contractor back home in Missouri and was in awe of the amount of work that had gone into building these villages, especially without the benefit of any kind of modern equipment. These villages couldn't be built today, he thought perversely, and just the idea of constructing something to last a thousand years was unimaginable. He even found it difficult to think in such terms.

Provence had been the first expansion of the Roman Empire north of the Alps. Around a couple of centuries B.C., Hannibal and his elephant corps took the Romans by surprise at Lake Trasimeno and gave them a pretty serious drubbing, almost changing the entire course of western history as a result. After the Romans recovered from the shock of Hannibal's unwelcome and unexpected visit, they realized that the Alps were not the formidable deterrent to invaders that they had thought and decided that they had better expand north and set up a new frontier.

True to their nature, the Romans built everything they could think of in the newly conquered territory. Then they built and built some more.

After a few more centuries and the eventual fall of the empire, raiders from the Eastern Mediterranean found out about all this incredible booty and repeatedly attacked and sacked this area of Provence. The local tribes responded by moving and rebuilding their villages on the sides of mountains, a defensive measure that put their enemies at a decided disadvantage.

After marching with their weapons and their heavy armor uphill for mile after mile, the barbarian invaders were so exhausted that the simple farmers could defend their villages with common garden tools. Sam pitied the poor barbarians, coming all that way with grand plans for mayhem and madness only to be frustrated by a few lowly peasants.

The Baker's objectives, however, were far less sinister than those of the ancient raiders. Their needs were simple: food, drink, showers, and sleep . . . in that order. A familiar routine had evolved over the days for finding these necessities. They had eventually developed a nose for scouting out a comfortable little chamber d'hote lodging and a local cafe to wash away the accumulated trail dust from some very dry throats.

The daily prospect of such refreshment and renewal had carried them through some very tough stretches. Blisters, strained muscles, falls, and extra miles added on because of occasionally losing their way, not only were challenges but became minor victories of sorts when they worked together as a team.

The small, medieval village of Bonnieux marked the end of their hike. The village straddled an old Roman road that climbed over the Luberon Mountain and eventually carved it way through the Provencal hills down to the Mediterranean Sea. Bonnieux began as a Roman outpost and later became the summer home to the Popes when they reigned at Avignon. In time, countless others - even the Knights Templar- came and left their mark. But today it was the Baker family's turn, their triumphal entry and a chance for a much needed rest. Today, Bonnieux was their Shangri La, spa resort, and pilgrimage destination all wrapped up in one.

 As they entered the village, Diane spotted a small sign for the lodgings that had been recommended by their previous host. Diane and Beth insisted on first going straight to the chambre d'hote complaining that their blistered feet needed immediate attention. Sam, however, having his own idea of how to finish the day, began looking for the nearest outdoor café. It seemed to him the only appropriate end to a hot and dusty day as well as a fitting way to celebrate completion of the entire hike.

The vision of a cold drink had been Sam's motivation and strength as the Provencal sun baked the last drop of moisture from his body on the seemingly endless road up the long hill to the village. They walked with heads down to avoid the intense glare of the sun, occasionally looking up to see the village shimmering mirage-like in the heat and getting closer at a discouragingly slow pace. But they trudged on, knowing that food and rest would eventually be their reward. It

6

was only a few hundred steps. Or was it a few thousand.

 Sam could appreciate Diane's and Beth's need for rest. His feet hurt too, but feet would just have to wait. It was his parched taste buds and dry lips that needed immediate attention. He owed it to his vision to follow through, he thought, and said goodbye to Diane and Beth at the steps up to the cafe and promised he'd be along shortly as soon as he had properly rehydrated himself.

The café at the top of the stairs looked similar to so many others they had seen in the past days as they walked from village to village and it fit Sam's exacting requirements perfectly . . .

 It was open.

 Village cafes were usually small, nondescript affairs with miniscule signs that required diligently searching out to make sure you weren't going into a butcher shop or the local car repair garage. But this one was pretty obviously a cafe or maybe his antennae were hypersensitive and could detect cold drink at a hundred paces.

This café conformed to French national tradition.   In
anything but the coldest weather, most patrons ate and
drank in the out-of-doors. The dining area was
furnished with small white plastic tables and chairs
huddled in cozy groups on a terrace in front of the café.
It reminded him of little islands awaiting private
rendezvous.

 The terrace was paved with miniature white stones
that gave a distinctive crunch with every step by patron
or waiter. Perhaps a warning system left over from the
middle-ages. Two gnarled plane trees brooded over the
whole space like giant umbrellas and provided a
welcome shade. Their dense foliage diluted and
diffused the sizzling Provencal sun to a cool, gray glow.
Sam's eyes needed several seconds to get used to the
dusky light before he ventured in.

He let his pack fall to the gravel with a thud and
dropped himself into the first chair he found.   When he
looked back over the valley they had just left, he could
finally appreciate the beauty of the countryside but
found it hard to imagine that the thin twisting ribbon in
the far distance was the road they had been tramping
on so wearily just a few hours ago.

Beyond the café's terrace, the medieval village wall, and

the red tile roofs of the nearby village houses, the view fell away to the broad plain shimmering in the late summer heat. A trickle of a stream flowed somewhere down there, splitting the valley in half, more a dividing line than a source of water.   The wines grown on one side of the all-but-dry stream were better than those produced on the other, Sam had learned; and the answer to which side was better depended on who one asked.

The patchwork of cherry orchards, olive groves, grape vines, and lavender fields spilled down the slopes weaving a dusty green carpet to cover and soften the ancient stone of the Luberon. The perfect setting, he thought, what could be better.

A tall, thin waiter wearing a white apron soon appeared out of the dark interior of the café and stood business-like beside Sam's table, bringing Sam's attention back to his thirst. Pen to pad, ready to take a seven course order the waiter asked,   "Vous avez choisi"?

Have I decided, Sam thought, you must be kidding. This decision had been made shortly after *petit déjeuner*.

 "Une pression, si'l vous plait", Sam said in his best

French, hoping that he'd made himself understood.
The waiter apparently did understand Sam's rusty
French as he turned and left like a man on a mission.
Sam wondered if he looked as tired as he felt. If he did,
maybe the waiter had sensed the opportunity for a
good tip and would get his beer in short order. He
could already taste it. The round paper coaster on the
table boasted *1664* to be the house brew - a French
beer made in the German style in Alsace, that most
German of French regions.

Alsace, like a valuable family heirloom, had been
contested back and forth between France and Germany
for well over two hundred years. The Alsatians fate
depended upon who had won the last war. The
architecture and food were decidedly German but the
people were definitely French in their outlook and
customs. A person's name could be either French or
German or a combination of both. The land was
beautiful and life revolved around grape growing and
wine making. The beer was just a bonus.

Sam's brief mental jaunt into Alsace was soon
interrupted by the waiter carrying a frothy, frosty glass
of *1664*. The glass touched the table for about a nano
second before Sam lifted it to his fevered lips and took a

long, cold, refreshing draft. He put the glass back down into the wet ring it had made on the table, slowly moving the glass in a circular motion as he listened to the waiter crunch away through the gravel. He closed his eyes to the intense Provencal light, savoring the wonderful taste and moved his tired body around in the chair trying to find the most comfortable position. He smiled to himself at the thought that he might remind anyone watching of a dog circling its bed before finally lying down.

As the cold liquid worked its magic, he reached down to his boots, loosened the strings and tried to quietly slip them off. Hopefully, this wasn't a social taboo in France but he had to get out of them even if for just a few minutes. He hadn't realized how much his size eleven feet hurt until he had addressed the problem of his thirst. His feet hadn't hurt like that since army boot camp. And of course, now they were carrying a somewhat heavier load. He was both jealous of Diane and admired her at the same time. After almost twenty years of marriage, she was still in great shape and could pound the trail like a marathoner.

Now Sam wished that Diane and Beth had stopped at

the café with him, wished that they could see that view. Maybe he'd go down to the little hotel and get them. Yes, he had decided, he would do that right after he finished his beer.

He still had on his sunglasses and figured no one would know he was sitting there with his eyes closed. That is, of course, unless he actually dosed off and fell out of his chair. He slowly raised his hand to his ball cap and tilted it down an extra notch just for insurance. Sam fought the urge to give in to the tiredness, the warm stir of the air and the relaxing effect of the cold beer and just take a little nap.

He lingered for several seconds in this drowsy neverland before a thought hit him. If Diane and Beth did come looking for him and found him slumped over in his cups sound asleep, he'd never hear the end of it. He straightened up a bit and reached for the glass, confident he could find it without having to open his tired eyes.

Instead of that cold glass, his hand settled on something dry and coarse feeling. He tensed. He was sure he'd knocked the glass off the table and now all he had was a handful of beer coaster. He hadn't heard the crunch of something landing in the gravel, but maybe he had actually dozed off and hadn't realized it. Sam strained to lift heavy eyelids and found his hand resting on a long paper tube of the kind used to mail posters and such. Not being at his mental peak and a bit groggy, it took a few seconds to realize that his beer hadn't morphed into a post office product. The tableware now included two items, one of which he'd ordered and one that had just appeared from nowhere.

He sat up straighter and looked around, wondering if someone nearby was watching for some comical reaction from him. It was a favorite Provencal café joke perhaps.   His first impulse was to yell out for Beth. She was fond of pulling little jokes on her father.

He sat up straighter and looked around at the nearby tables.   Three others were occupied. Couples seemed deep in private conversations, leaned in on elbows, intense concentration on each other, totally unaware of him. He could have been another one of the tables as far as they had noticed.

 He looked toward the adjacent car park. A rangy dog sniffed at something on the pavement and a small gimpy-legged man was climbing into an old and dusty green Renault fifty yards away. Sam looked toward the waiter who was standing just outside the café entrance, still in his stiff pose. Surely he must have seen who put the paper tube on his table, Sam thought, since he seemed to be watching the terrace with the eye of a hawk, instantly ready to refill a glass or write out l'addition. He grabbed the tube and crunched through the gravel in his socks to where the waiter stood guard.

" Voudriez-vous encore de pression," the waiter asked hopefully as he approached. With the waiter's rapid-fire speech and his own concentration on the paper tube, Sam hadn't understood the waiter's question,

"Pardon", Sam said.

The waiter shrugged and with a smile asked in English, "Would you like another beer, monsieur?"

"Non, merci," Sam sputtered, "maybe later."   He thrust the tube at the waiter. "Did you see who put this on my table"? The waiter looked down at the tube and then back at Sam. And then at Sam's bootless feet before finally answering

"Mais oui, monsieur, "his right arm rose and hung in the air like one of the trail signs that Sam had seen so many of in recent days. His eyes followed the line of the

waiter's arm, past his brown hand and bony finger –
straight to the parking area. He saw the backside of the
old Renault as it sputtered away, disappearing behind a
cloud of diesel fumes - a magician's trick complete with
magic smoke .

Chapter two

Louis Jaubert leaned on the rough stone kitchen sink and looked out through the dusty window of the rustic old bastide, or farmhouse, that he had rented a few days before. His wary eye searched the horizon for some sign of his visitor, a visitor that he had been expecting for over an hour. He wasn't too concerned yet, but to have his plan put off schedule - even by a little bit - gave him an uncomfortable twinge in his stomach. But after all, this was Provence, a land where few worried about schedules. And of course who would ever know but him, Louis Jaubert, a few rabbits and the hawk that circled lazily overhead. That's why he had picked this old farmhouse.

 He'd stumbled on it by accident and was taken by the idea that anyone would build a house in so remote a place. He quickly realized how it could fit into his plans and rented it from its elderly owner for cash, a pittance. He was quite sure that the tax man would never hear of their arrangement and in fact, he doubted if anyone would hear of it – to know that he was there, other than the old man and some trusted friends. It was perfect for what Louis had in mind. He wanted to be away from the cottage, Mama, and Marguerite for their safety.

Louis, a careful man, had no qualms with engaging in certain activities but liked to keep his distance just in the event a problem arose unexpectedly. And since he was a careful man who planned every detail, the chance of a surprise problem was slim….. but one never knew.

The driveway to the bastide was long, rutted , and dusty, and invited no casual visitor. It was a back road off a back road deep in the Luberon, stretched out like a long brown finger, its arthritic-like bends eventually connecting to a country lane just over a rise of low shaggy hills. The high Luberon was the perfect haven for anyone needing privacy. A maze of hills and gorges, cliffs and caves, this land could swallow up anyone wanting to get away from civilization for whatever reason.

The old farmhouse itself was a badly rundown affair.   It had seen the ravages of at least two centuries of punishing Provencal summers and winters. What didn't dry up in the summer heat and blow away in the Mistral, froze in winters cold and blew away on that season's frigid wind.

17

The low one story house was almost hidden in a saddle between two hump-like hills on the Luberon landscape. To repair something like this – just to make it habitable again - would eat up a small fortune. At best, it could be described as a fixer-upper. In truth, it was a ruin. It had nothing to attract unwanted attention. Louis liked it that way.

He had been waiting a long time for this moment. He smiled to himself at the thought of the old building and the fact that it needed a considerable number of repairs. In the few days he had been there, he had come to feel something of a kinship with the old place. He, Louis Jaubert, could also use some updating and renovation, and like the old house, he too had a certain character, if a bit shabby. Maybe he should buy the old house and give it a real overhaul. He laughed out loud at the thought.   He'd soon have the fortune to do it with, and more.   Much more.

Laughing made the little creases at the corners of his mouth almost connect with those around his eyes, the overall look being one of careful satisfaction. For two long years Louis Jaubert had carefully planned what he had to admit even to himself – and only to himself – to be a master stroke, a certain 'activity' that would soon make him a very rich man. Just the thought of it made him smile again although it was against his nature to count his successes before they actually happened.

Nevertheless, it was a very pleasant thought and he decided at that very moment that he would just buy the old house when it was all over. "Yes", he said out loud as if to confirm it to himself. He would buy the old place. A man needed to own property at least once in his life.

Still searching the horizon, Louis found his gaze drawn away from the window and toward the cracked mirror that hung lopsidedly beside the old lace curtain. He was surprised when he felt something like disappointment with the worn and slightly haggard image looking back at him. He hoped that most of the defects belonged to the mirror, but in many ways Louis was an honest man and knew that a good many of those defects were his own. Perhaps along with the old house he'd get himself into better shape.

He was a man of a certain age who had enjoyed too much good French food too often. And since he wasn't a man who enjoyed sweating at his work, he didn't get much exercise. Over the years the pounds had crept on and the muscles had gone a bit flabby. Marguerite had never complained but one day had simply walked out the door with her suitcase. Rumor had it that she had taken a fancy to some sharp-eyed little gendarme in Cavaillon. Later he heard that she had moved in with him.

 Louis had not given too much thought as to why she had gone and had not seen her in over a year.   He had not felt too much grief at her leaving and saw it as just a sad but natural and acceptable part of life's journey, at least his journey.

Now with no wife, he saw even fewer reasons to change his habits. But he knew that what he was planning would definitely change his life, one way or the other. His life would either take a much higher road or slide back into the hellish pit at Marseille. He knew that he was afraid of failing but was surprised at his own lack of real excitement with the prospect of success.   That is, until the plump little baker's assistant had begun to smile at him when he made his daily visit to the village boulangerie for croissants.

She wasn't what he would call pretty nor was she all that young. But somehow the tiny beads of perspiration trickling down the deep cleavage that showed as she retrieved hot bread from the huge oven gave her an appeal that he couldn't explain.

20

He thought of her with every bite of his croissant. With the fortune that was so nearly his, he would get himself in shape and take her away from the hot work of the boulangerie. He'd lose a few pounds and visit some of the fancy fashion shops in Avignon. Women always appreciated men who dressed well. He'd never been able to afford fashionable clothes before but that was about to change. And of course, she would look even better in some new clothes of her own. He was sure she would be most appreciative. He felt equally sure that it just wasn't being near the oven that made her . . . . .oh well, he could think more about that later. A smile tugged at the corners of his mouth. He might even buy that shiny new Peugeot that he had admired for so long.

As he waited by the window, a distant rumble pulled his thoughts away from the image in the mirror to the cloud of dust on the road connecting his drive to the D road.   It had to be Jo coming to report completion of his part in Louis' plan.

 Louis' smile widened ever so slightly when he was finally able to identify Jo's old green Renault as the source of the dust, bouncing along the rutted dirt track between a neglected vineyard and an equally run down cherry orchard.   His smile also reflected a little draining

21

away of the tension that had crept in when Jo hadn't shown up on time.   He hated having to depend on his nephew but he wasn't about to make direct contact with the buyers for what he had to offer. If something went wrong, he wanted to be somewhere else. He felt guilty for using his own nephew as a buffer, but the boy needed to work and didn't seem suited to too high an occupation.

Jo was simple- minded but had proven trustworthy in simple affairs. But alas, he often needed reminding that schedules were made for a reason and that keeping to them was most important to the successful completion of their kind of work. Louis remembered with a bit more guilt, that Jo had acquired his gimpy leg in his uncle's service by jumping from a second floor window when he had been late leaving a job. But the boy was family and family had to be looked after. There was also the fact that Louis needed an errand boy. That allowed him to do what he did best – to plan and direct.

He heard the old Renault cough and shamble to a stop. The car door slammed with a bang that rattled the bastide's loose and neglected windowpanes. The crunch and drag cadence of Jo's crazy walk up the gravel path announced his arrival at the front door.

Jaubert moved quickly for a big man, covering the few steps to the front of the house. He barely pulled back the dingy lace curtain to check that Jo was alone before the door burst open. Jo stood there half in-half out with his sun toughened face wearing a silly lopsided grin.

Louis let go of the pent-up tension and felt the muscles around his shoulders relax just a little. Jo was late but everything was ok. The poor dumb kid would never make a poker player, his face gave away his every thought. Jo's big grin told him that the delivery had been successfully made, but Louis still felt the need to growl at his nephew a little just to keep discipline up. Jo wasn't the brightest of the boys he employed so sometimes a little yelling helped to keep his attention.

Before Jo could say "Bonjour, Uncle Louis," Jaubert barked at him and made the smaller man jump.

"Where have you been? Why are you late?

Jo's sense of satisfaction couldn't be dampened and through the still-in-place grin he said, "I was stopped by the gendarmes on the Route 100."

Louis' heart almost jumped from his chest. His knees

felt rubbery and his will to discipline Jo had been replaced by cold fear and dread. It required all his will to find his voice, "Did they find the tube"?

"No," Jo said, shaking his head so hard that his grin seemed to slosh around his face like a water-filled balloon. "It was just a traffic check but it took me a while to find my papers. Since I can't lock my old car, I have to hide them and I forgot where I put them."

Louis was almost afraid to ask his next question, "But you did get there on time and make the delivery, oui? You actually gave him the tube?"

"Oui, Uncle Louis, he was still there at the first table looking just as you described him. Ball cap, sunglasses…..tres Americaine, oui?

Louis wanted to tell Jo that the man who wanted to buy his painting was a Russian pretending to be an American. That was just the way Russians thought - everything had to be cloak and dagger, too complicated to try to explain to Jo.

But Louis was so relieved and angry at the same time that all he could do was to clamp his jaws together, nod his head, and sit heavily onto one of the rickety chairs that passed for furnishings in the old house. He wasn't sure whether it was better to choke Jo or hug him. Get this close to being rich and a man of his age didn't need such scares.

Just as his heart began to slow down from its thumping and he could think about smiling again, his cell phone shrilled and made them both jump.

"Monsieur Jaubert," the voice was cold and hard like Luberon limestone. Louis was immediately on his feet.

"Oui", said Jaubert. It was the call he had been expecting but something felt decidedly wrong. The voice did not sound like it belonged to a man prepared to pay him an obscene amount of Euros for a small picture, no matter who's name was on it.

"We had an agreement. My man waited but no one came. This is not the way I do business". The hard Russian accent made each word sound a threat. Louis' courage faltered for a brief moment. A tiny tremor wobbled one knee and he shifted his weight. He felt as if he were waiting for a bomb to explode.

But Louis Jaubert was a careful man and collected himself admirably, "Neither do I, Monsieur, neither do I. A thousand pardons. I wish to conclude this transaction as much as you. Patience, si'l vous plait, monsieur.

25

Jaubert was filling up the phone line with words, wondering what could have happened, wanting to gain time to think what Jo could have done wrong, " Give me until the evening to set things right. I suspect a small error has occurred that can be easily righted."

"Eight o'clock", the Russian voice growled in agreement. But Louis heard it as an ultimatum. One he wasn't sure he would be able to meet. His first impulse was to choke Jo and then deal with the disaster, but he didn't have the time. It was for situations like this that he did all the detailed planning. He put his big arm around Jo's shoulder and after mightily resisting the urge to crush his whole body, simply said, "go home boy, I'll call you when I need you." The next words were even tougher to get out but the boy needed encouragement, "Good work, boy, good work."

Louis knew there was nothing more to be found out by grilling Jo or in asking him to go over his movements again. Jo had already told the story as completely as he knew how.

Jo seemed in no way curious about the phone conversation and left the old house with his grin still in place. Even the shuffling gait was a little crisper, thought Louis. Maybe the little fool was already starting to think about spending his part. Louis waited until the old Renault was kicking up another cloud of dust up on the vineyard road and the clatter of the worn diesel had quieted to no more than the buzz of a cigale. He moved back from the window, turned and walked toward the scarred and worn table with its collection of odd chairs – probably abandoned when the previous occupant had left because it wasn't worth taking.

He sat back down heavily, propped his chin on his fist and absently looked about the room. What had happened? He wondered. In a panic, he had told the Russian that a small error had occurred that could be easily righted. He had no idea what had happened; how could he know how to fix it? He made a point of mentally reviewing each step to think where the problem had crept into his plan. This was supposed to be the easy part, the payoff.

Actually the easy part had been stealing -that is, acquiring - the painting. Everyone, even the museum curators and art experts agreed that, regrettably, not a single Cezanne of any real value still existed anywhere in all of Provence. Regrettable, because Cezanne had been born in Aix-en-Provence and had lived there most of his incredibly productive life. He had even committed his impressions of one local mountain, St. Victoire, to canvas over seventy times. And now all these precious French jewels were scattered around the world – nothing of importance left in the land of its birth.

 All the experts agreed.

 Louis Jaubert knew better.

Chapter three

Louis had grown up in a derelict little village a few
kilometers to the south of Aix. Le Pont D'Avont was a
farming village that had long past seen its better days.
With the village well past its prime, some of its more
prosperous land owners had occasionally tried to revive
their little town and made an attempt at growing wine
grapes. Unfortunately, Le Pont D'Avont and its environs
was one of the few places in France that grew grapes
suitable only for making vinegar.

After so many failures, they had neither the stamina,
the courage, nor the resources to try anything else. Le
Pont D'Avont had shriveled like an old man, unable to
do what he once did in his youth, and waited quietly
and helplessly for the inevitable.

The Jaubert home was a small and Spartan two-room
cottage just at the edge of Le Pont D'Avont. It had been
part of a larger estate presided over by a chateau of
respectable size. The owner of the chateau had fallen
into financial ruin and had deserted the estate during
the depression. Abandoned, the stately old building
had quietly but steadily slipped into a state of ruin.

29

The Jaubert cottage and several others on the property became like satellites of a dead sun. His mother had watched the old place closely just to see what would become of it. Not that she would ever want to live there; it was simply a matter of curiosity, and mama Jaubert's curiosity was matched only by her diligence in trying to satisfy it.

Soon after the Great War, she had told him, a strange couple had come to live at the chateau. They were never seen in the village and only rarely glimpsed at the chateau. Occasionally a big car would drive up to the front of the chateau and its passenger would hurry to the door, be admitted and then leave again within an hour. Sometimes mama could see that they carried a package; sometimes, nothing. No one ever stayed long.

Whoever they were, the couple slowly and quietly brought the old house back from the brink and by the time Louis was old enough to notice, it resembled so many other old houses around Provence – a gracefully aging old dowager. Certainly nothing like a restoration to its previous state but at least the slide into total dilapidation had been arrested.

As a young man, finding nothing to do in Le Pont D'Avont and little more to keep him occupied in Aix ,

Louis took himself off to Marseilles. He worked hard for a few years around the docks before falling in with three brothers who had developed a way of making a living without the inconvenience of having to work for it. Everything had gone well for the first few years and Louis had become quite taken with the ease and comfort of his new lifestyle. It was far easier than the backbreaking work he had been used to on the docks and he was now able to send a few francs home each month to his old mother. Louis was her only family and she would struggle except for his help.

Sometimes Louis even thought he should be with her there in Le Pont D'Avont but what good was his company if he had no work and no way to put the few francs in her tattered old purse each month. After dealing with these occasional bouts of guilt, Louis would put such sentimental feelings behind him for he knew he liked his life in Marseille. The money was good and the work was not at all taxing.

However, many businesses eventually suffer an occasional rough spot and the three brothers' little enterprise was no exception. They decided to cut overhead and needed a scapegoat for a particular plan that had gone sour and had attracted the unwanted

31

attention of the local gendarmes.   With blood being thicker than water, Louis was elected in a landslide vote. Unfortunately, the loss of his job turned out to be the least of Louis' problems. All fingers pointed toward him when the Marseille police began asking some very rough and painful questions.

 In all truth, Louis knew none of the answers, but he spent the next twelve years trying to figure exactly what had gone wrong and living as a 'guest' of La République Francaise.

Louis often thought about home and Aix and wondered why he had been such a fool in his youth. Why had he rushed off to Marseille. Surely Aix would have held some opportunity for him had he just tried. Why had his life turned out as it had.

 He wondered what divide in the road had turned him from the pleasant green valley to the bleak and wretched desert. He wondered how a man's life could be moving in one direction and a moment later be picked up like a leaf in the Mistral wind and tossed helplessly about, unable to stop the madness and get a new footing.

 More often though, he simply thought about how long

a time twelve years was – how long it had already been and how long it was yet to be.

He thought a lot about what he would do when his time was finally finished. He dreamed about Spain and wondered what life and work would be like there. Occasionally, he thought that he might go to Sicily with a friend.

He spent hours thinking of other places that would be pleasant and dreamed about life in the cities, in the mountains, or in some warm and tranquil seaside village. He was certain that he, Louis Jaubert, would appreciate these places more than its natives ever possibly could. But wherever it was to be - when he was allowed - he'd be out of Marseille within an hour, maybe sooner.

Actually, the more he thought about it, the more his thoughts seemed to turn time and again to the same question. What was in Spain or Sicily for him? More wandering? Perhaps more trouble? Almost certainly he would be alone. The more he thought about his future, the more often he realized that a nameless force tugged at him, urging him in the same direction. He recognized it and took some comfort in its familiarity. He would offer no resistance. He reckoned he'd just go back to

Aix and settle in with his old mother. She'd need someone in her helpless days.

 God bless her, he thought, she had written him faithfully and often and would prattle on for pages about the simple doings of the village, the neighbors, and even Aix whenever she could manage to scrape up bus fare to visit the city. She was like a sponge – she would absorb the local gossip and rumors and repeat it all for Louis. It was a lifeline for him, a thin thread anchoring him to sanity and reality. Her meanderings were entertaining and rambled through and around any subject that caught her fancy.

Mostly, though, she was fascinated by the old couple who lived in the nearby chateau. She had all kinds of crazy theories about who they were. Once she was convinced that they were deposed royalty from some small and insignificant eastern country. She imagined all kinds of strange customs being observed at the chateau and several times heard the eerie sounds of what she swore were wolves baying.

 She wasn't in the least discouraged in her investigations when she later found the unearthly noise was nothing more than a neighbor's hunting hounds becoming excited over the scent of some small animal out on its nocturnal rounds. She would often walk as closely by the old chateau as she thought she could without arousing attention, looking for evidence of her suspicions.

Later she came to believe that the lord of the manor was a retired crime lord from Corsica. Curious traffic in and out of the place was almost certain proof of such. Why else would long and shiny black automobiles wheel down the plane tree lined boulevard connecting the chateau to the main road at the most unusual hours. Whatever her theory d'jour, it kept him entertained, relatively sane and helped pass the hours and the days and the months and the years.

Eventually, one of her letters brought news that the old man had died. She found out only from querying the postman, the one person in the village with a healthier curiosity than Mama. Mama had noticed that one of the huge black cars had come down the boulevard raising a white cloud of dust and parked close to the big double doors at the front of the chateau. Two men had carried out a long and –from the way they struggled - evidently heavy load and soon drove swiftly away. What could it be but the remains of the Monsieur himself. She was certain.

There had been no mass, no last rites, no nothing. It wasn't right she thought. The postman agreed. He had developed the habit of personally delivering the mail to the door of the chateau, a new service of the French Poste, he had explained. Actually the French Poste would do nothing of the sort, but it allowed him to satisfy his own enormous curiosity and then share any juicy news with Mama Jaubert. She, in turn, would always fill in the blanks for the postman in his own keen inquiries into village life.

This news was a good opportunity to satisfy her curiosity even more, she stopped by the chateau soon after to pay her 'respects' and found the old lady in a very grievous state. She also found the house to be unbelievably lavish on the inside – opulent even; the total opposite of the worn looking exterior.

A hint of a smile formed under Louis' bushy mustache when he thought that that description also fit Mama so well. With a threadbare apron tied up over a plain black dress, Mama had a worn looking exterior, but inside was a lively spark that in better opportunities could have blazed to a much brighter flame.

Louis' mama was quick to put this new information to

good use and volunteered to help the old lady through her trials and grief. Mama soon became indispensible around the old chateau and fired off frequent letters to Louis with all kinds of new speculations.

 Louis especially enjoyed this sequel to Mama's earlier letters but he was pleased even more to know that she now had something of a purpose in her life.   It seemed that now with the monsieur gone, the madam was willing to spend a little money to get help around the big old chateau and had put Mama on a regular stipend. Mama had assumed the roles of laundress, housekeeper, and cook, and relished her unofficial post as foreign correspondent to Louis.

 The old madam eventually hired a nice looking woman from a nearby village to take some of the load off poor overworked mama Jaubert. Mama hadn't objected to the hiring and may even have been somewhat responsible because of her frequent hints and declarations of excessive tiredness.

The new woman, Marguerite, was younger and could drive and so assumed the duties of chauffeur. Never having learned to drive herself, the madam of the chateau saw this as a welcome opportunity to get out of the old pile of stone – something the monsieur, while

37

he was alive, had apparently forbidden or at least strongly discouraged.

Mama Jaubert saw a somewhat different opportunity. While Marguerite was driving the madam around the Provencal countryside, Mama Jaubert was conducting an informal survey of the old chateau and making a mental inventory of things that could have some value to certain merchants in Aix.

When Louis finally came home from Marseilles after so many years, Mama Jaubert had a couple of surprises waiting for him. Mama suggested that Marguerite would make him an excellent wife and that the old lament that there were no worthwhile Cezannes left in all of Provence – accepted by almost everyone, certainly was not true.

There was at least one.

It hung on the back wall of Madame's boudoir, right between a small Picasso and a Dufy. With the extra money she'd earned at the chateau, Mama had taken the bus into Aix and spent many afternoons at libraries and museums becoming quite knowledgeable about certain artists. She had decided that the Cezanne was the best candidate for a new idea that had been

38

cooking away in her mind. The main reason was, if everyone thought there were no Cezannes left anywhere in Provence, why should it ever be missed if it suddenly disappeared.

Over the years, the plan had taken root and grown steadily in Mama's devious old mind. It required, however, waiting until Louis came home to put into action. Mama had also learned something else through diligent digging and studying. It was a secret that apparently only Mama was privy to, and that secret was the very key to making the whole plan work.

Louis thought about that secret and took heart. Everything would be ok. Mama was always an inspiration. She'd taught him to keep quiet and keep his eyes open to opportunities. From her he'd learned the importance of planning, even to having other sets of eyes watching over his efforts.

 He reached for his cell phone and punched in Paulo's number. Paulo was the smartest of the crew that Louis had put together for this job and was dependable and loyal. They had known each other for the last seven years of his involuntary stay in Marseilles. In fact, they had seen each other every day of that time, had listened to each other snore through the long nights.

Louis shook off the awful memory. The tough little Sicilian answered on the second ring. He had been waiting for the call.

"Oui", the economy of words was Paulo's trademark

"Louis here," said Jaubert. Before he could ask the question he had been afraid to ask, Paulo got right to the point, "Boss, I think there may be a problem."

"Go on", Jaubert said, with the twinge in his stomach beginning to sound its warning again.

"The Russian's pickup man was on time and waited for almost half an hour," Paulo said.   "Jo never showed. The guy seemed pretty nervous and looked at his watch a lot and finally just got up and left. Left his drink on the table; never touched it. I waited so see if he'd come back but he didn't. The waiter finally decided that he wasn't coming back and cleared away the drink.

 Soon, another guy came along and sat at the same table. Same get up again – American ball cap and big sunglasses. He hadn't been there for more than a couple of minutes when Jo finally hobbles in, dropped the package and kept sailing. The guy didn't pick it up for a minute or two and didn't seem to notice Jo. I actually think the guy was taking a siesta at the table.

Then when he did finally see the package on the table, he looked surprised, glanced around several times and then went up to the waiter and must have asked him who had put the package on his table because the waiter pointed toward Jo as he drove off. If he was the right guy, why did he go through all that?"

Louis thought about it but didn't answer. Instead he said hopefully, "You did follow the second guy, oui?"

"No boss, I followed the package"

"Bon, Paulo, great work." Louis had given Paulo in this job because he had shown he could think on his feet when things didn't go exactly according to plan.

"Where is the package," asked Louis.

"Well, that's the next funny part. He left the tube on the table. I was about to pick it up when he comes bounding back up the stairs. He grabbed it, tucked it under his arm, and headed back down. I was ready to follow him in my car but he didn't leave the village. Instead he walked down to the little hotel at the bottom of the steps and went in. I made a call and found out that he's checked in there – with a wife and a kid."

"Merde," said Louis, "get some sleep and be back early

just in case they're early risers. Stay with them. We've got to get it back."

"Oui, boss. Looks like they hiked in and the only way out is to hike or maybe take a taxi. A friend drives with the local taxi service. I gave him ten Euros and asked him to let me know if the guy called."   Paulo was off the line.

Louis stood and walked back to the kitchen. He leaned on the rough stone sink and put his face as close to the window as he could. The cloud of dust made by the old Renault had long settled and in the still, clear air a scarlet and ocre band drifted lazily over the hills. He watched as the Sun slid over the horizon and made its daily exit from Provence. He loved the simple beauty of a sunset in this land, a pleasure he had missed so many times at Marseille. Buoyed by the pure joy of watching it now, he was able to face an unpleasant task. The call had to be made.   He didn't like talking to the Russian, but now they were the ones with money. He felt better after talking to Paulo. Things were under control again. It was still going to work and Mama would be proud.

 He punched the Russian's number into his cell phone and waited for the ring.

42

Chapter Four

Sam turned back to the waiter, who gave him a shrug but no further answer.   He paid his check, picked up his pack and hurried down the steps to the hotel. Half way down he remembered that he had left the paper tube and whatever it contained on the table. For a half second, he thought about going on since the tube really wasn't his and he had no idea what could be in it. Probably some prank. But something in his curious nature made him go back for a second look.

When he got to the top of the stairs, Sam saw a lean, dark man walking toward the table where he had been sitting. When he saw Sam, the man hesitated a step, glanced at the tube and then back at Sam. For a moment, Sam could sense that the man thought about reaching for the tube, but then he walked away after giving it another brief look and kept going toward the café.

 Sam went to the table, picked up the tube, tucked it under his arm, baguette style, and turned back down the stairs. At the hotel, he found the proprietor, got the room number and practically bounded up the long set of stairs, ready to share his strange encounter with Diane and Beth. One tap on the door and Beth swept it open with a "Dad, where have you been"?

The question was evidently rhetorical and neither she nor her mother seemed to be interested in Sam's answer. He sensed something else was afoot.

He looked from Beth to Diane who had the same conspiratorial look. "I've just checked on the Internet" Diane said, "and the hotel we wanted to stay at in Avignon for a couple of days does have a room available for tonight."

"But we have a room for tonight. We're standing in it!" Sam said, suddenly too tired to think of doing what they were thinking of doing.

"We could be there in an hour, find a wonderful little restaurant for dinner, and sleep in tomorrow morning," Diane added.

Sam figured that they had already made the decision and were just testing him to see how much resistance he'd put up.

"But we've already paid for this room . . . haven't we?" he tried again.

44

"We've only been here ten minutes, haven't made any mess and I'd bet that if we offered to pay something, they'd be happy to take it and try to rent it again." Diane said in what sounded like a closing argument.

"Ok," Sam surrendered, "I'll see the proprietor and ask him to call a taxi". Truthfully, he was a bit anxious himself to see a little city life after so many days in the countryside.

It wasn't until they were in the cab that Beth and Diane noticed - and Sam remembered - that he was carrying his unusual package.

"What's that?" asked Beth, reaching for the mailing tube without waiting for Sam's answer

"I don't know", he said, and surprised himself that he had been carrying it around for so long without knowing what it was.

"Where did you get it," Diane wanted to know. Sam lifted his shoulders, pushed out his lower lip and gave her the Gallic shrug that he had become so adept at in a short two weeks. Diane started to ask again but decided to wait, her attention now on Beth.

Beth pulled the plastic caps from both ends and held it

up to the waning light as the taxi drove toward the Papal city of Avignon. She pushed a finger into one end and saw a rolled up paper appear at the other. She pulled it out, spread it across her lap and looked at it for several seconds before a puff of air escaped her rounded lips followed by an emphatic 'Wow!'

Diane leaned over for a better look and Sam waited, unable to see anything but the back of what looked like a canvas from the front seat. They both waited for something after the wow. With no reaction but seeing her eyebrows climb her forehead, both said 'what', in unison.

"This painting looks so real and it's signed!" Beth said nothing more as if that finished her analysis and answered all questions.

"Signed ?" Sam asked. "Who?"

She turned it around to face him and as his eyes searched the strangely familiar style and brushwork, he saw the signature in tall swoopy letters . . . Cezanne.

"Where did you get this," Diane asked.

Sam told them the whole - if short - story as to how he had come by the tube with its canvas contents.

"Why didn't you stop the guy?" Beth asked as if such a thing should have been so obvious, "and ask him why he gave it to you."

When Sam didn't answer right away, Diane looked right through his defenses and in her best public prosecutor voice, said, "You were sitting there dozing, weren't you."

"Guilty, your counsellorship", Sam pled.

"So, what are you going to do with it?" Diane began her line of follow-up questions.

Sam tried to deflect her curiosity since he was way behind in the answers department, "Would you stop being a prosecutor for a while. You're on vacation. We'll figure it out later. I'm hungry. We're going to be in Avignon in a few minutes. Let's think about restaurants."

Beth still had the canvas stretched out on her lap and was studying it intently. "This doesn't look like the stuff you can buy in the tourist shops. It looks really old. It's a little dirty and the paint's cracked." Her mouth dropped open, "Do you think it could really be…."

"Of course not, "Diane said , "the question isn't *what*

47

but *why* . No matter what it is, why would someone just give it to your father. Didn't that strike you as a little unusual, Sam, especially since he didn't say anything. Why didn't you just leave it there?

Sam was feeling a little stung by Diane's tone, "OK, so I was napping.   I've been walking all day and was just a bit tired. And I took it because I'm a curious sort and saw no sinister plot behind the whole thing."

"I'm sorry, "Diane said, "I didn't mean to say you did anything wrong. I was just wondering why you left it and then decided to go back after it."

Sam stared out the window.

Beth said, "But isn't it possible that it might be…"

Before she could finish her thought, Diane punctured her fantasy, "Sure, and when we get to Avignon, Dad can be the Pope."

Sam turned back from the window and deadpanned, "No thanks, I have enough problems of my own." They all laughed. The tension was broken and Sam assured them that they'd all work it out in the morning after they had rested. He noticed through the lowering twilight that they were already in the suburbs of

Avignon.   Diane pulled out a guide book for Avignon and began to read off the must see and must do attractions of the ancient city. They forgot about the canvas and began to concentrate on their growling stomachs. Lunch had been an apple and a piece of hard cheese and breakfast had been a dozen hours ago.

The cab driver parried with other traffic and swerved through the narrow streets barely missing pedestrians and miraculously escaping their own destruction under the wheels of huge trucks and buses. In Sam's view it really was a miracle, but the cabbie finally got them to the address Diane had given him and within minutes they had checked in at the hotel.

 Soon after, they were back out on the streets of Avignon and were tempted into a little restaurant on the Place d' Horologue. The strings of twinkling lights in the plane trees above the dining terrace and the incredible aroma coming from a platter that a waiter delivered to a nearby table got immediate agreement from all three as the perfect place for dinner.

The majestic bulk of the Papal Palace- now bathed in moon-white light hovered over the main square of Avignon as it had for half a millennium. A few cigales played their rasping tunes from the nearby trees as

49

strollers wandered arm in arm through the cobblestoned square.   Dinner lasted almost past their ability to stay awake and over the last few bites of a spectacular crème <u>brûlée</u>, they decided to stay for a couple of days in Avignon, then rent a car, visit Aix-en-Provence, and have a couple of days on the beach at the pretty little fishing village of Cassis before heading back home to America.

As they walked back to the hotel, the three of them were feeling very mellow as the result of consuming a liter of very good Cote de Luberon red. Diane put her arm through Sam's and said, "Aren't you glad that we came on to Avignon tonight."

"Sure," Sam agreed, "That was a pretty spectacular meal and it's good to be back in civilization."

 While Sam was being agreeable, Diane thought she'd try another question. "Now, aren't you also glad that you came to France with your family instead of doing something silly with your juvenile friends."

Sam smiled, "Ok, I concede. They can be juvenile sometimes, but what's silly about mule trekking in the Grand Canyon?"

Diane started to answer that but didn't. They had

discussed this at length for weeks before Sam finally put the guys on hold and decided to do another of his family's long distance walks. No more discussion was needed so they were content to walk arm in arm and watch Beth ahead of them as she excitedly took in the evening street scene. The sounds of concertinas and violins floated through the summer evening air along with the aromas of herbs and spices and grilled meats – Avignon was a flood on the senses.

Sam loved his family, but was a little bored by the walking day after day. He had wanted to do an adventure vacation. Get a little excitement in his life. Being a builder usually lacked in the thrills department, so when the guys mentioned giving up their annual golfing trip for a special adventure in the Grand Canyon, Sam mentally signed on and immediately began thinking of a way to get out of going to France. The resulting discussions hadn't always ended without some slightly wounded feelings on one or the other's part. Accommodation was finally reached and another long distance walk was in the Baker family history book.

He had to admit that getting in shape felt good even if the first two or three days almost killed him. Sam liked having Diane's arm through his and watching Beth

51

ahead. He gave a little sigh, smiled to himself, and
thought 'next year'.

Chapter five

Louis Jaubert heard the bell ringing through the fog of sleep. Persistent. Incessant. Demanding that he wake up and get dressed. Every morning he was required to present himself at the door of his cell, to stand there at attention until the guards did their inspection. It was 6:00 A.M. Time for roll-call. They wanted to be sure that he was still here, he thought with perverse irony, *and where else would he be? Where else had he been for the last 4,380 days?* Louis began to roll himself toward the side of the bed and his half-open eyes met the red glow of his alarm clock. It read 8:42.

Panic gripped him and a cold sweat bathed his forehead before his feet could hit the floor. He was late. There would be punishment. Though his bewilderment lasted only for a moment, it was long enough to set both hands to trembling. He buried his face in his unsteady hands and imagined that he saw the despairing image of his old mother looking at him, silently crying out his name, tears streaming down the deep furrows of her cheeks. He had disappointed Mama again. He tried to calm his rattled nerves.

Looking about, he realized that he was no longer in that awful place in Marseilles. *Merci, mon Dieu*. His relief was like a reprieve from the gallows. He was well acquainted with this cycle of fear and relief; the dream came too often and felt too real.

The ramshakle walls and floors and ceiling of the old bastide now seemed a mansion to him. He gave his head a shake to clear away the ugly dream.

The bell was still ringing. It was his cell phone. He reached for it with one hand and pulled a sleeve across his forehead with the other. His arm came away with the dark stain of sweat. He looked at it and wondered how a man could react so totally and so quickly to fear, but the answer to that he knew all too well.

His mouth was dry . . .tongue, lips and teeth all stuck in one useless mass. He grunted a weak "Oui" into the phone and picked up the glass on the bedside table. He'd never before tasted Pastis this early in the morning, but he needed it to settle his nerves. He swallowed the dregs of last night's drink and listened.

"Boss, it's Paulo. I got a call from my friend at the taxi service this morning. Said he took the American and his family to Avignon last night. They checked into a little hotel near the Pont d'Avignon - Auberge St. Remy. Took the room for a couple of days."

Louis got the name that the American had checked in under and thanked Paulo.

"Good work, my friend. Soon we'll be rich and can sleep until noon – every day". He said it as much for self-assurance as for encouragement to Paulo. He briefly thought of asking Paulo if he ever had dreams about Marseille. He didn't. Louis knew the answer to that too without asking. He also knew that Paulo wasn't like so many of the others he had known at Marseille. Like Louis, Paulo had done some stupid things in his youth and had paid the price several times over. Louis wanted his plan to work out for Paulo almost as much as for himself and Mama and Jo.

Louis looked at the phone and promised himself that he would change the ring tone before it could make that awful sound again. He quietly dressed and walked into the musty old kitchen and found what he needed to make coffee. While the pot bubbled and whistled toward the strong, caffeine laden brew he desperately needed, he went to every window, pulled back the soiled and frayed curtains. He stood to the side of each window and cautiously surveyed the horizon.

A quiet peaceful countryside lay behind each curtain, an idealized painting framed by each window; its only inhabitants, vines and trees. No gendarmes surrounding the house, no snarling black dogs straining at their leashes, jaws snapping open and shut, ready to break bones – his bones. By long habit, Louis' hand went down to his thigh and felt the scars - holes really - where huge teeth had ripped at his flesh so many years ago. Or was it only yesterday. Just the thought of that horrible experience brought an involuntary shiver. He waited for the spasm to pass. Satisfied, he stood back from the window. Caution was even more important now.

He went back to the kitchen, took the half finished pot off the stove and poured himself a cup. As the coffee coursed through his system, he began to feel calmer. His hand no longer shook - he hated that feeling. He sipped at the strong black liquid, elixir for his nerves, and held the cup at eye level as if to toast their success, but it was really to assure himself that his hand was indeed now steady. He rubbed his thigh while he thought.

Refilling the cup, he played back in his mind what Paulo had said. *The American and his family went to Avignon last night*. Strange. They had already checked into the local hotel – and then suddenly left. That concerned him. Could they know what it was that they had in their possession. Could they be aware that only by a dumb mistake had a simpleton dumped a thing of such sublime beauty and incredible worth into their laps? Did they know the truth and were they now running away with his painting? Or was this just another example of the strange things that Americans were often known for doing.

If they knew and intended to keep what was his, why would they go no further than Avignon? They surely would have fled to Paris or Bordeaux; some place far away from Bonnieux and the mistake that had left it in their possession. But if they really intended to stay in Avignon for a few days, it meant that they had no clue about what they had and were most likely just tourists planning to do tourist things. Avignon was a magnet for people like that. The Germans, the Dutch, and the British swarmed over this part of Provence every summer like bees over the lavender fields. And now it was the Americans adding to the crowds.

Whatever they had planned, it would get them out of their room and away from his painting. This was the break he needed. He would send Jo to watch. He

57

wondered what the American was thinking about having something like this just dumped in his lap while he was trying to sleep.

When the American and his family went out, Jo could let himself into their room and retrieve what rightfully belonged to Louis Jaubert.

Louis smiled at the thought. Jo would love this. He would march right up to the innkeeper, sure to attract attention with his stumbling walk, flip out the old city inspector badge that he had bought at a vide grenier - flea market - and bluff his way in. But with that thought, a barely felt twinge fired its warning in the middle of his stomach again. Should he send Paulo instead? His gut said not to trust Jo on this assignment, but his heart said to give the boy another chance, after all, he was family. This should be easy, straightforward. Nothing to get complicated. Besides, he had something else that required Paulo's skills. Louis picked up his cell phone to call Jo. Before he went to the call list, he scrolled down to *ring tone* and hit *change*.

Chapter Six

The Bakers slept late as planned. After *une petite dejeuner* of flaky croissants topped with melted *fromage de chèvre* and a coffee that must have been brewed by the angels, they stepped out into a brilliant Provencal day and onto a very busy sidewalk. The crowds were already building in the old city of Avignon.

The narrow sidewalks reverberated with a dozen languages as travelers from all over Europe and America, Africa and Asia jostled each other, anxious to see everything and enjoy everything the city of the Popes had to offer. Street performers vied for their attention and scores of regular vendors hawked every imaginable product from soaps to santons, cheap watches to huge bolts of Provencal fabrics, from exotic foods to every kind of clothing. Everything needed to sustain life.

It was market day in Avignon.

The aromas of coffee, bakery products, the spicy smell of dried sausages, the ubiquitous scent of lavender, the tang of chestnuts roasting over charcoal fires, all mixed

59

together, a euphoric assault on the senses , the essence of the French *joie de vivre* every visitor came looking for.

Sam could imagine that some things hadn't changed all that much since the 15th century when the Popes would stare down from a palace window onto this same square, watching their subjects do the same things they had done for centuries past. But politics changed and the Popes had long ago taken themselves, their courts and their hangers-on back to Rome. Still, some vestige of the majesty and mystery of Peter's successors lived on in Avignon like a ghost unwilling to give up its ancestral home to uninvited interlopers. The magic was palpable. Sam and his family let themselves be carried along with the crowds.

Beth had wanted to take the canvas to a gallery or two just for an opinion but Diane and Sam convinced her that they would probably be laughed right out of the places. No need to invite embarrassment. They decided, instead, to visit the Palais des Papes. Sam had thought that it looked so magnificent last evening from their dinner spot that he suggested it as their first tourist activity. Beth and Diane made it unanimous.

The lively atmosphere of the city, the sharp, intense

blue of the Provencal sky, and the lingering satisfaction of a delicious breakfast had Beth, Diane, and Sam in a generally affable and happy mood right up until they arrived at the ticket window of the Palais des Papes. Sam reached for his wallet and found an empty pocket. He immediately went into the comedic pocket slapping act where both hands are flapping like a wounded bird, patting each pocket, in turn , to find out which held his mislaid valuables.

"What are you doing, Sam," Diane wanted to know. But she immediately realized the problem. "You don't have your wallet, do you?" she said as if talking to a small child who habitually forgot everything.

After a moment of panic, thinking that he had been the victim of a pickpocket, Sam remembered that he had slipped his wallet under the mattress of their bed while the family went for breakfast. He couldn't remember why he had done that and felt a bit sheepish. That feeling was compensated for, however, by the comfort of knowing where it was, that it hadn't been stolen. It wouldn't help to ask either Beth or Diane for a temporary loan, because their travel policy was that only he would carry the family's money. Two fewer people to lose something. Sam was beginning to see some flaws in that strategy. Beth and Diane gave him

61

looks that were a mix of accusation and pity. Diane shook her head, and then smiled. "You're hopeless, but I'm going to keep you."

"OK, it's not that far back to the hotel," Sam said. Wait here, window shop and I'll be back in fifteen minutes." He started back along the Rue de la Balance before they could begin a serious debate on his qualifications as family treasurer. He stopped in mid-stride, reached into his pocket, turned back, and gave them the few euro coins he had. "Get some coffee, I'll be back in a few minutes."

Sam zigged and zagged through the crowds and got to the hotel in seven minutes flat. He felt good about his estimate for getting back. They'd get into the next tour of the palace and he was sure he'd be forgiven. He wedged myself into the tiny elevator and impatiently waited for it to inch its way up to the fourth floor. 'Left out of the elevator and to the end of the corridor,' he repeated to himself. Door straight ahead. He stopped in front of their door and reached into his pocket for the key. As he was about to put it into the lock, he noticed that the door was slightly ajar. Ouch, he thought, he was glad he had come back by himself. He was the last one out and now, he would have to add leaving the door open to his crime spree. He'd be in for a real reprimand – and in real trouble if anything were missing.

He tried the knob. He not only hadn't closed the door, he hadn't even locked it. He pushed it open and went to the side of the bed, knelt on one knee and reached his hand into the area between mattress and springs and felt the comforting bulk of his wallet. He felt relieved.

The next thing Sam felt was an immense explosion in the back of his head followed by brilliant fireworks behind his eyes. The room spun and tilted sidewise. His consciousness slipped away like a medieval ghost gliding out the door.

Chapter Seven

 Jo arrived back at the bastide, his hands shaking so violently that he had barely held the wheel of the old Renault straight, struggling to keep it between the ditches of the narrow country lanes. Thankfully he had not passed a single car on his way back. The realization of what he had done burned into his brain and fear quickly turned to panic.

Louis heard the old Renault slide to a stop in the gravel. He hurried to the front door and checked through a narrow part in the curtains. He could swear that Jo was coming up the path so quickly that he had no time to limp. The look on his face said something was terribly wrong. *Mon Dieu*, thought Louis, *what's happened now. I knew I shouldn't have sent him*.

Jo charged right past Louis into the house, dropped into one of the rickety dining chairs and laced his fingers together behind his neck, his head down and rocked back and forth. His bad leg was slewed to the side. A groan came from somewhere deep down and Louis knew that something awful had Jo in its grip. Louis quickly pulled up another of the chairs facing Jo and waited – afraid to ask. He ran his thick fingers through his hair and felt the same desperation that showed in Jo's tormented body.

 "What's happened, boy", he wished he could cover his ears and not hear the answer. Ever since the old lady of the chateau had herself succumbed to old age, he had dreamed of this moment – converting a real Cezanne into a lot of real cash. Doing something especially nice for Mama Jaubert. He didn't want her to have to work anymore. She was way too old for that.

 And now something was going to ruin all his dreams, even to spoil all his hopes for Jo and Paulo – and for himself . . . and that plump little baker's assistant. He could see all these visions taking flight, never to be realized as he had once expected. And it just wasn't a prize lost but there would be a penalty to be paid. Louis tried to put this thought out of his mind and steel himself for what might be next.

The secret that mama had learned while working at the chateau had made him so confident of his plan. One day while Marguerite was driving the old lady down to Marseilles, mama had found some documents that changed everything. No longer would they need to worry about what would happen to them when the old lady was gone. What mama had learned meant that all they had to do was wait until she was gone. And now, the dream was dying like the old lady.

 He put his big hands on both Jo's shoulders and shook hard. "Talk to me boy, what's happened."

Jo looked up and with big tears flowing down his anguished face, said "I had to hit him, Uncle Louis. He fell down and wouldn't move. His head was bleeding. I waited a long time, but he never moved". Jo was sobbing now. "I had to get out of there. I couldn't stay with him lying there like that."

Icy fingers clutched at Louis' heart. He couldn't imagine that his plan would ever have come to this point – violence. He had experienced the nightmares of Marseille. Never would he want to be the perpetrator.

 "What do you mean, you had to hit him. Why did you have to hit him. Speak, boy, for God's sake. Talk to me." He shook Jo again.

"I looked everywhere in the room but there was no tube. I looked everywhere, Uncle Louis, everywhere. I was standing there trying to think what to do next –

66

what you'd want me to do - and then I heard somebody turning the doorknob. I jumped back behind the door. The American came in and knelt down next to the bed like he was going to pray or something.   But he reached under the mattress and pulled something out and started to get up. I knew he'd find me and he's a lot bigger than I am. So I picked up the closest thing, a lamp, and hit him.

He just fell down and never moved. He never made a sound. You don't think he's . . . . " Jo sobbed and began to rock back and forth again.

Louis closed his eyes and saw ghosts of Marseilles. *Don't give up yet,* he told himself. Maybe he's not badly hurt, just knocked silly for a while. He'd send Paulo to see just how bad things were.

However bad things might be in Avignon, they seemed even bleaker here at the bastide. He'd have to call the Russian and ask for more time. And pray that the American was not dead.

Chapter Eight

What's happened to my head, Sam asked himself
through a painful fog. His head was pounding like it was
being used it for jackhammer practice. Everything in his
vision was dancing around in triplicate.

When he woke - which wasn't really an accurate term -
he was on his knees with his head jammed under the
bed. His first impression was that he had been hit by
one of the big trucks that charged down the narrow
streets of Avignon like the bulls of Pamplona and he
was still trapped under it.

When his head cleared enough to realize that he could
move, he pulled himself painfully and slowly out of its
clutches. His whole body rolled over onto his back.
Sam now sat with both legs splayed out, his neck bent
at a worrisome angle, arms hanging at his sides, not
obeying any commands sent by his befuddled brain.

He had blood on both hands, his shirt, and felt a
warmth trickling down his back. Sam looked at the red
stains on his hands and clothes and had no clue as to
whose it might be or how it had got there. It didn't

occur to him that he should be concerned. His wallet lay on the floor beside him. That's strange, he thought, I don't remember putting it there.

Sam laid there immobile for a long time. He felt desperately thirsty but was afraid that if he moved, the receding roar in his head would erupt again, complete with more fireworks. Then he heard footfalls in the hallway and voices. Somebody was coming to rescue him. Or perhaps, to push him back under the truck, this time to finish the job.

He wondered in a strangely calm way why someone wanted to run over him. He knew he should get up and try to defend himself, but his limbs would not respond to his brain's call to action. The door opened and Sam blinked and felt unbelievable relief. There stood the two most beautiful women in the world.

Amidst very startled looks and muted screams, they flew to his aid, one on each side holding his limp, bloody hands. He could see huge tears welling up in Beth's eyes, "what's happened, Dad. Are you OK?

Not quite, he thought calmly. He seemed to be floating above the scene assessing the strange events, an impartial observer. Diane left for just a second and was back with a glass of water and a wet towel. She started to wash his hands. By now, he had associated the blood on his hands with the pain in the back of his head. He took a little sip of water and sat up just a bit when the roar in his head started all over again. But it was Beth screaming. She had seen the bloody, matted hair on the back of his head.

Diane motioned her to the door, "Go have them call a doctor." In a flash, Beth was gone.

Sam now saw that Diane was sporting a couple of big tears rolling down her cheeks. "Can you talk? Can you tell me what happened? Say something, please!

"I think I'm ok," he mumbled, not too convincingly. "I don't know what happened. I guess I just fell somehow." He was starting to feel better not having to look at his own blood. "Thank you for doing this." He knew that Diane didn't like seeing blood and usually looked ready to faint at the first drop.

Footfalls in the hallway again – many feet this time, hurrying. Sam braced again.

The proprietor hurried in with another man he introduced as l'docteur Fournier. Beth was right behind, looking a bit relieved to see her father a little more tucked in and cleaned up.

The doctor set a small black bag on the carpet beside Sam and quickly set about to determine Sam's condition. He looked from Sam to the broken lamp on the floor and quickly added two and two and arrived at a reasonably accurate sum. He reached into his bag, brought out a small black cylinder, pushed a switch and shot a beam of light into each of Sam's eyes, and pronounced both pupils to be of equal size.

After checking the back of Sam's head and asking a few more questions, he declared that Sam would most likely live if he didn't repeat his most recent activities. He made Diane and Beth promise to keep a close watch on the patient and take him immediately to a hospital should he begin displaying any unusual symptoms. Before the doctor could list the possible warning signs to look for, the hotel owner gave a sharp gasp, "Merde," he said, sounding shocked and getting everyone's attention, "What has happened to the room?"

They followed his gaze around the room, seeing for the first time the disorder that engulfed every part of the room except for the spot where Sam lay stretched out. Every suitcase was emptied with their clothes scattered about. All drawers were open, some tossed on the floor. Closet doors open, pillows torn apart. Sam had, apparently, walked in on a robbery in progress.

Despite the damage done to his property, the hotel owner was reluctant to send for the police. "Monsieur, you probably don't want to be bothered by the gendarmes," he suggested, "They ask a thousand questions and never catch the villains. And you look like you need some rest. I'll have someone clean this up and I'll move you to another room, d'accord?" Without waiting for anyone's approval, he was out the door.

That was ok with Sam. He needed time to process all this. After the hotel man and doctor left,   Beth and Diane set about putting things back in order. Sam pulled himself into a chair and sat looking over the damage.

 "Whoever did this wasn't just looking to steal things in general," Sam said. His wallet with a couple hundred euros in it still lay on the floor, Beth's laptop computer, still open on the bureau top.

 It slowly dawned on him that the cardboard tube with its rolled up canvas might have been what they were after. He looked about as well as a stiffening neck would let him. It wasn't there. "The tube and canvas are gone," he said to Diane and Beth. "That's what they were after. Somebody wanted the painting back."

"The painting's not gone," said Beth. "I had it in my day pack. I know what you both said, but I put it in my pack when we went out this morning. I thought that if we were anywhere near a gallery that we could maybe stop in and just ask. If they laughed . . . . so what."

Diane turned and looked worriedly at Sam. "If they didn't find what they were looking for, do you think they'll come back?"

"Maybe," he said, "And we shouldn't be here when they do….. must have been twenty or thirty of them," he tried to lighten the mood without much success.

"I hope the owner hasn't gone to a lot of trouble with another room," Diane fretted.

"Actually he might be happy to see us go, Sam said. Less wear and tear on his hotel."

With Diane and Beth's help, he finally managed to regain his feet. "This checking out early is getting to be a bad habit," he gave it another try and grinned.

Beth gave him a weak smile and said, "He's going to be ok, mom, he's trying to crack a joke."

When Diane and Beth had got things back into some semblance of order, Sam sent Beth down to tell the owner that they'd be checking out. Diane continued to clean up the back of his head.

 "Doesn't look too bad," she said, "Just a small bump but a pretty good cut. That explains all the blood. You really didn't want to go to the Papal Palace, did you?"

"You can see right through me, I'm afraid," Sam said. They both laughed. Relieved.

"Seriously, Sam, what are we going to do about this thing . . . this canvas. It's trouble. It's dangerous."

"Well, I think Beth's right. If possible, we need to find out if it's more than what I think it is. Is it a ten euro piece of kitsch or is it something really valuable. Is it worth enough for someone to go around,"   Sam swallowed hard when he actually put it into words, "breaking into hotel rooms and bashing people on the head."

He could see that what he'd just said amounted to proof - circumstantial evidence of bad intent - to his public prosecutor wife.

"You're right," she said, "if somebody took the risk of breaking in here and assaulting you, this canvas must have a lot of value. But that still doesn't answer the question – what are we going to do with it? And an even better question is why do we have it in the first place?"

Beth came back into the room and caught the tail end of their conversation, "He didn't really seem to mind that we were leaving."

Sam wasn't surprised.

"I have an idea," Beth said as she opened her suitcase and took out her laptop again. "I remembered from an art history project at school that there's an internet site where you can find out if a particular artist has any paintings on a missing or stolen list."

"What makes you think is might be stolen," Sam asked

"Dad," she drew the word out, exasperated that he hadn't fully grasped her train of thought. "If the person who did this really owned it, would they have to break into our room and whack you on the head?"

"Oh," he said. His fog still not totally cleared. He looked from Diane to Beth for an answer.

"So you think that whoever dropped this on my table might have stolen it? But why? Why give it to….." He stopped. It was making his head hurt worse to think about it.

Beth went through several web sites about stolen art, missing art and weird art. The amount of art stolen each year was astonishing. The F.B.I estimated that the annual value of stolen art was over 6 billion dollars. Beth worked through web sites like a combination investigator/electronics guru. She finally arrived at one specific to works of the impressionists and post impressionists. Cezanne seemed to fit somewhere in this broad category. Each tap of the mouse pad brought a different painting onto the laptops screen.

It seemed that Cezanne was responsible for a substantial part of that 6 billion. Picture after picture stolen from private collections, museums, college endowments, and government offices. Finally, one tap on the computer was followed by a collective intake of air. All three immediately recognized that the picture on the computers screen was identical to the canvas stretched out on the bed. They looked at each other, at the canvas, and back at the computer. A brief notation next to the picture identified it as "The Chateau". On the next line it added, "believed to have been confiscated by Nazi's from private collection, Karlovy Vary, Czechosolavakia, July, 1942."

No one said anything. Nobody knew what to say.

Beth started tapping the computers keys again furiously.

"What are you doing now," Diane asked.

Beth didn't answer, just kept typing.

"There," she said. "There's where we need to go."

Diane and Sam leaned in to look at the screen. It was the web site for an art museum in Aix-en-Provence – Le Brabet.

Chapter Nine

Louis Jaubert was on his fourth cup of a fierce expresso. His hands were doing a steady twitch which made it hard to hold the cup, and interfered with thinking things through. It was partly the caffeine, but Louis knew that the disaster brought on by Jo was the real culprit. He not only had failed to return with the canvas but had complicated matters with a real crime. Then insult was heaped on top of this blow when he had telephoned the Russian again.

It was the second time in two days that he had wanted to throttle Jo, but Louis couldn't bring himself to be too harsh and had to admit that it really came down to his own mistake. He should not have sent Jo to Avignon. It was a job beyond the boy's capabilities and Louis should have admitted that. He should have gone himself, but he had allowed the idea of 'family' to get in the way of good judgment. "Keep the boy busy", mama always said. "He needs the work." Both Louis and Mama always referred to Jo as 'the boy' although he already into his thirties. She felt a strong responsibility for her nephew. Her only sister, now departed, hadn't provided the boy with much direction, nor had he seemed able to absorb what small amount had been offered.

Mama Jaubert hadn't said as much, but Louis sensed that she held him to blame for Jo's handicap. I didn't tell him to jump from a second floor window, Louis thought in his own defense. The boy's just too careless. Louis himself, through much painful experience, had become a very cautious man. Many headaches could be avoided by being careful. He wryly wondered if the American would agree.

Then he remembered as the chipped cup and saucer rattled in his hand and he worried that the American might even be dead. "Mon Dieu, No, s'il vous plait" he pleaded under his breath.

Louis realized his mistake was just that – a mistake – not a plotted crime. He hoped it could be corrected. Of course if he had gone himself, he could have been there when the big American came in and then maybe he would be the one with the bashed head. No, things could be worse.

Louis had sent Jo back to the little cottage on the grounds of the chateau to wait for the outcome – whatever that might be. The thought of failure suggested so many dark consequences. He might never see Mama Jaubert again. Without him and the successful completion of their plan, she would live a pauper's existence or have to bend her old body to drudgery until she wore herself out. And he wouldn't be going for any more croissants. He wouldn't have any hope of seeing that plump baker's assistant except in his dreams. He and Paulo could end up back in Marseilles . . . . a thought that sent a violent spasm through his already trembling hands.

 His fifth cup of expresso landed on the table, chards of china and thick, hot liquid splattering his lap. Louis looked at the shattered cup and saw an image of his life. Too many pieces to put back together, maybe it would be easier to sweep it all into the trash bin and forget.

Jo's fowl-up had been bad enough but that damned Russian had added the coup de grace. Louis had called him a second time and explained that he had sorted out the problem with the painting and that it was only a matter of hours until it would be available for his inspection . And, Louis hoped, to be exchanged shortly for a vast quantity of Euros. They had already agreed on a testing and authentication procedure.

In the silence that greeted him he could sense the insolence, the arrogance that only a nouveau riche barbarian could display. His only other encounter with a Russian had been that bullying Muscovite, Badovich, who like Louis had found himself an unwilling guest of the République Francais in Marseilles.

 Badovich had the nasty habit of cursing everything French and somehow blaming Louis for the details. Prison had been bad enough by itself, but with someone like Badovich stalking him at every turn, it had been hellish. Louis had no idea why he had been targeted by the Russian.   Paulo, too had felt the bad end of Badovich's temper and found that friendship with Louis worked in both their best interest.

It was here that Louis began to see the wisdom his old mother preached – keep your eyes open and your mouth shut. And plan carefully. Such efforts by Louis – a secret gleaned here, a word in the right ear there – had landed Badovich in solitary confinement. In Marseille prison, where the dregs of the Mediterranean criminal culture mixed like a vile and poisonous brew, solitary confinement meant a black hole of a dungeon that rarely saw anyone come out a whole man. Louis' success in ridding himself of Badovich was generally acknowledged by the rest of the prison population and

had also made him a hero to many others who hated
the Russian.

But now it seemed that Badovich had gotten retribution
through a countryman. Why were they all so brash and
haughty, Louis wondered.

 The Russian had cut him off with a crude remark when
he tried to explain and ask for just a little extra time. He
didn't care for Jaubert's problems and considered the
complications the result of stupidity. And he was sure
that with all the mistakes, Interpol, and every other
police agency in the country was already sniffing
around, ready to grab the painting and send everyone
involved away for the rest of their miserable lives.

The Russian swore at Louis and said he no longer
wanted the painting, Cezanne or not. It was now
tainted and that ruined the value. If Jaubert ever did
get it back, the Russian rudely laughed, he'd buy it for a
hundred Euros. Otherwise, Jaubert could take his
painting and stick it up his French arse.

Louis was shocked. He felt pummeled and bruised.
He'd lost his buyer, Jo was now a useless member of the
team, and all their dreams were falling over a precipice,
never to be reclaimed, smashed below on the rocks of

his stupidity. The Russian was right, and to have to admit that, hurt Louis almost as much as the fact that he was letting Mama down.

His cell phone rang. If all his worst fears were coming true, it could be the final blow. He'd have to leave France, but how. He'd be a wanted man in all the European union countries. Maybe he could make it to North Africa. No, he dismissed that idea straight away. He'd rather stay in France and take his chances. The phone continued to taunt. He thought of the American. What was the penalty for . . . .

He pushed the answer button. "Oui"

"Boss, it's Paulo."

Louis listened, ready for the worst.

"The American is ok, got a bandage on his head, but walking around." Paulo said.

Louis' relief was papable. He collapsed in relief into one of the old straight-backed chairs hard enough to break it, but it held. The American was alive. Louis looked up at the ceiling and muttered a heart-felt "Merci beaucoup." They wouldn't be able to add that charge to his account.

"So he's actually walking around, he's Ok?", he recovered at this good news. "Did you see the picture?"

"I saw the tube," Paulo answered, "The girl was carrying it. They've checked out of the hotel early again. I was afraid that meant they were leaving the country but they took a cab to the train station and rented a car. I followed them onto the motorway but lost them at the toll plaza. They were heading towards Aix."

"Good job, Paulo. Go on to Aix and see what you can find out."

"Boss, one more thing. I asked a few questions, quiet like, around the hotel. Funny thing, the gendarmes never came. If they were ever called, they never showed up." Paulo thought again about something odd that the hotel man had said, the shift in his eyes. He added, "They were probably never called."

Louis wanted to thank Paulo . . . . no to hug him. His call was like salve on a wound. The American was OK but

Louis wondered why he hadn't called the police. He would have if someone had broken into his room and hit him on the head. But then again, if he were in possession of a Cezanne that wasn't his, knew what it was, and had just enough larceny in his heart to think about keeping it, he probably wouldn't.

That was good, Louis thought, having the flics sniffing around just complicated his job in getting the painting back. He'd had a little bit of luck; something had turned his way.

Louis almost felt like smiling, until he realized that the American probably knew too much.

Chapter Ten

"What exactly do we say to the people at the museum," Diane asked, as they approached Aix on the A8 motorway. "Do we ask, 'what is this and can we keep it.'"

"Of course we keep it," Sam dead panned, "I've paid for it with a huge lump on my head,"

"You two, "Beth said in mock seriousness. "We just tell them how you got it and let them figure it out from there. Then we can go to the beach."

It was a pleasure for Sam to be zipping along the autoroute at the wheel of a quick little Peugeot instead of slogging along a narrow trail on foot. Instead of watching for steep drop-offs and wild boars charging across the trail all he had to do was avoid massive trucks and try to keep up with the frantic traffic.

It also helped take his mind off his headache and the problem about the painting. Diane and Beth seemed caught up in their own thoughts and Sam simply watched the Provencal countryside slide by as grape vines and cypresses slowly gave way to small factories and apartment buildings. They were approaching the outskirts of Aix-en-Provence.

They held reservations at an Aix hotel near the Rotunde, but with their recent penchant for short stays, were now three days early. A quick call before setting out from Avignon and they found that wouldn't be a problem. A room could be ready.

They checked in, left the tube in the hotel safe, and spent the next hour walking along the Cours Mirabeau, Aix's equivalent of Paris' Champs Élysées. The street was a wide and elegant thoroughfare made just for leisurely strolling. It was lined on one side with shops and cafes and on the other with a few banks sprinkled among a long row of patrician townhomes, quaintly known in French as l'hotel particuliers.'

One end of the Cours Mirabeau was anchored by the Rotunde, a traffic circle with its own huge fountain, and the other by a statue of a legendary Provencal monarch, the Good King Rene. It was shaded along its entire course by giant plane trees, giving the impression that the Cours Mirabeau was a long and leafy, green tunnel.

Making this whole scene look industrious and happy were hundreds of people who appeared to have nothing else to do but lounge at sidewalk cafes, drinking wine and enjoying animated conversations . Hands cut through the air like an artist flinging paint against a giant canvas, shoulders hunched and fell , and the hum of conversation and laughter rung through it all with an intensity that could be felt as well as heard.   All this against a backdrop of swerving, groaning and honking cars, trucks, buses and mopeds.

Aix had all the *verve de vie* of Paris spiced with the warmth and languid texture of the South.

It also had tens of thousands of university students adding to the general din and exuberance. The American family immediately fell in love with the city and decided that here there would be no early checkout.

Diane was primed with information from the travel guide she'd read while Sam drove and nursed a tender neck and head. She quickly spotted the café where, for centuries, both notables and nobody's had found sustenance, plotted revolutions, and generally enjoyed the good life. She decided that it would be suitable for them, too.

Le Deux Garcons was the favorite of generations of

literary and artistic icons such as Hemingway, Zola, and even Cezanne himself. Over the centuries, there had been a long parade of movie stars and politicians as well.

They found a tiny table right by the sidewalk and enjoyed a wonderful and relaxing dinner. With the fright and the excitement of the morning, this was just the perfect way to get them all down from adrenaline highs.

Their dinner began with an amuse bouche – something to amuse the mouth. Then came the entrees and main courses, salads, cheeses, desserts, and coffee. After a few days of eating like this, Sam thought he was beginning to detect a little tightness around the waist but another bite of the silky chocolate mousse helped dispel such unpleasant thoughts.

Unwilling, or perhaps just unable to move, they nursed a second carafe of the local wine until dusk began to create purple shadows along the boulevard. Overhead, lights wrapped around the branches of the plane trees began to twinkle on and an altogether different kind of magic took hold. A never ending parade of humanity served as live entertainment and Aix took on an aire of splendid indolence as it settled into its evening persona.

Diane and Beth talked about their just finished walk and how much they had enjoyed it as a family. The events of the morning began to ease into the background a little and they were finally able to relax.

Sam was unusually quiet as he listened to his family talk. His headache had slowed to a gentle throb, and he felt they were safe among the crowds of gentle diners, strollers and people just enjoying life and each other.

Diane wanted to ask Sam again if he was happy that he had come to France with them instead of going on that silly "guys" trip, but after the events of the morning decided not to. But they did need to talk about their present problem.

"Just what are we going to say to the museum people tomorrow," she asked for the second time.

"I think that Beth is right." Sam said. "I'll simply tell them that it was dropped in my lap by unknown person or persons and, *viola*, here it is.

"So you think that will work," she persisted in her best cross examination manner.

"Why wouldn't it," he said, "It's the truth." He certainly didn't want to embellish the story and cause a bigger problem. He would have to think seriously as to whether he would even mention the whack on the head episode in Avignon.

As if reading his mind, Diane put her wine glass down on the table a bit harder than Sam thought necessary, looked straight into his eyes and said, "You're not going to tell them about what happened to you at Avignon, are you?"

He had decided. "No", he said.

Diane's look said she didn't agree with him.

Beth had been listening to their exchange and decided to cut off any further discussion. "There were some street musicians setting up at one of the cafes; could we stop on the way back and listen for a little while?"

They were now back in unanimous agreement and strolled along with the happy thought that they'd drop the painting off at the museum in the morning, enjoy another day in Aix and head off to the Mediterranean and its beaches.

Next morning, the sky above Aix had opened and an unexpected downpour drummed on their hotel window. It beat in rhythm with the drum in Sam's head. Unfortunately, the doctor in Avignon had forgotten to warn him about abstaining from wine until his head had healed a bit.

Diane and Beth, now cheated of their 'beautiful day' in Aix were not their usually cheerful selves. In this generally dark mood, they went down to breakfast and after an almost wordless half hour, went out into the grey dawn and sloshed through the wet streets to the Brabet.

The museum was an unimposing block of a building that sat as anchor in one of Aix's great squares. Except for a small tarnished bronze plaque economically announcing 'Le Brabet', it could have gone unnoticed, not looking at all the home of valuable works of art. They climbed a low set of steps and pushed through ancient and heavy wooden doors to find themselves alone in a cavernous entry hall. The high ceiling and the stone floors echoed their wet slappy footfalls and gave the place a forlorn feel.

They seemed to be the only people interested in visiting the museum that morning but it was early and Aix- like almost all other cities - lost much of its appeal under grey, wet skies.

The only thing that arrived dry was the tube with its mysterious contents. Sam had wrapped it in a plastic sheet and buried it in Beth's pack. After a quarter-mile walk through the rain, the three of them could have passed for circus clowns after a thirty minute water fight.

The guard at the Brabet regarded them with genuine pity. 'What could possibly bring you out in this weather,' his look said.

When Sam asked to see the Director of the Museum, however, the guard's countenance stiffened. "That is not possible, monsieur, le directeur is a very busy man."

Sam looked around at the empty and neglected room and wondered what the director could be so busy doing. There was no evidence of any excessive exertions by the director or anyone else. "It possibly concerns the whereabouts of a stolen Cezanne," Sam tried to sound nonchalant.

The guard studied Sam as if trying to decide if he was some crackpot that he should toss back into the rain but then held up an index finger to indicate that they should wait and disappeared through a heavy metal door.

"See how easy that was," Sam said to Diane.

They looked at some of the museums brochures while they waited and decided that despite first impressions, they had indeed come to the right place to return the painting. There were some minor Cezannes in the museum's collection and the native son was obviously held to be an artistic icon of the highest degree

The door opened again. The guard came through and stood to the side, holding the door open. Shortly, another man stepped through the door. He was a small man. An off-the-rack suit hung loosely on his thin frame, and his dark hair was in full retreat from his forehead. A bristly black mustache was the only distinguishing feature of his face save a wary expression that gave him a feral look.

He motioned to Sam without a greeting and indicated that they should follow him. The guard closed the door, made locking sounds and was soon at their heels.

They followed the director up two flights of stairs at a quick pace. Sam was glad that their recent hike allowed him to keep up and at the same time wondered if the place had an elevator.

He had never been in a museum director's office

before, but was surprised at the haggard look of the place. The director motioned them towards two chairs and took his place behind an oversized but worn desk.

The desktop had nothing to indicate that anything of great artistic importance was carried on there and was generally devoid of the usual office items except for an old pushbutton phone with a dozen red buttons along the bottom. It reminded Sam of the White House red phone in a cheap doomsday movie.

Diane and Beth took the two chairs and Sam stood between them. The director looked up at Sam but made no apology for the lack of sufficient seating.

He sat down at the big desk and stacked his hands one on top of the other giving the impression that he was either hiding something there or ready to conduct a séance. He raised one hand to put on a pair of heavy black-framed glasses and then slid them down his thin nose just enough to peer at them over the top.

"Madam, Madmoiselle, Monsieur, I'm afraid I don't have very much time" he waited long enough for that unfriendly bit of information to sink in, "So what can I do for you," his demeanor as charming as the weather.

Sam held out his hand to Beth. She dug in her pack and pulled out the tube. He took it from her, unwrapped the plastic cover, and took the two steps to the director's desk. He removed both endcaps from the tube and laid it on the center of the desk.

The director looked up at Sam without any change of expression, picked up the tube, held it vertically and gave it a good shake. The canvas dropped down enough for him to grasp it and pull it the rest of the way out. He flattened on the desk and looked at it for only a few seconds. His demeanor, like the guard's, did an about face. A hint of a smile began to transform the dark features. It wasn't exactly a friendly look and Sam thought he saw the mustache twitch.

Sam told him the story as simply as possible. Overnight, he'd decided that Diane was right and that he would include the part about Avignon after all. While Sam talked, the director examined the canvas brush stroke by brush stroke.

Sam couldn't tell if the director believed what he was saying or even if he understood. Sam's French wasn't exactly up to this kind of conversation. Beth tried to help, but the director never gave any indication of listening to her.

96

Without taking his gaze from the canvas he picked up the phone, tapped one of the buttons, spewed out an incomprehensible torrent in French, and returned it to the cradle. His concentration seemed to increase by the minute. They waited as he stared intently at the painting; no clues given on his face as to what thoughts were going on behind those glasses.

Finally a different guard came to the door. The director stood from his chair, crossed to where the guard waited and with his back to the Bakers had a private conversation, none of which Sam could hear. The director returned to his desk with his smile still in place. Now though, it looked as if he were having to work to keep it there.

He carefully smoothed out the canvas again, looked at Sam again and said "Un moment, Monsieur, si'l vous plait. I have to be sure"

Be sure of what, Sam thought, I'm not asking you to buy it. Sam looked from Diane to Beth, both had puzzled looks and Sam could imagine what was going on in their heads.

After several more minutes of watching the Director study every fiber of the canvas, Sam was about to say that they'd be going when a hard knock came at the door where the guard stood, arms crossed over his chest. The director nodded for the guard to open the door.

Two uniformed policemen strode into the museum directors office. Without a word or an introduction, both officers stared hard at Sam, Diane and Beth. Their dark eyes and the hard lines of their mouths were distinctly unfriendly and gave Sam an uneasy feeling. He looked at Diane and Beth. The same reaction showed in their faces.

The officer apparently in charge briefly acknowledged the director and then looked back toward Sam. "Monsieur, you and your family must come with us." He said it in a manner that was meant to discourage argument.

Sam looked back at Diane and then at Beth and started to protest until he saw the other officer conspicuously move his hand until it was resting on his sidearm. There was no mistaking the intent; the little cop had a sneer to go along with the move. A sneer that said, 'just try something, monsieur.' Taken aback by the gesture, Sam turned to the Director who he was sure could clear up whatever confusion there might be.

But with his smile now gone and the wary look back, the director stood and took a step back from his desk, "You must go with these officers, Monsieur, art theft is a very serious matter in France."

Chapter Eleven

The old bastide, a quiet hideaway tucked among the vines and empty fields, was a good place to sit and think and wait – and remember. A place to be quiet and turn over a problem in one's mind and look at it from all sides. Sometimes a different view could help clear up a mystery or at least suggest a different approach to finding the answer.

But Louis Jaubert was starting to worry that he had gotten in over his head. He had had this feeling before and it wasn't one that he was comfortable with.

When he came back from Marseille, he had started to work down Mama's list, a catalogue of certain things of value around the old chateau that Mama thought the old madam might not miss too much should they disappear.

A little vase here, a small piece of furniture from the hoard of things in the attic, or a silver plate that the old woman never, ever used. Louis had worked on the list for so long that it had begun to feel like a regular job. He would select something from the list and Marguerite would suggest taking Madam for a long drive in the country. Madam was always thrilled by the idea and she and Marguerite would be gone for the rest of the day. Louis would then take the *selection du jour* and drive the ancient Peugeot he had finally been able to afford into Aix.

The weekly markets in Aix with hundreds of sellers and thousands of buyers was the perfect place to turn these small items into much needed cash. Louis had carefully developed a small but obliging group of antique dealers who were happy to pay a reasonable price and who wouldn't think of inquiring about an items provenance, especially since most of the pieces Louis brought were of unusually good quality and rarely seen in this part of France.

It was a very agreeable situation for everyone concerned. All transactions were in cash so the vexation and inconvenience of taxes was never an issue. Not that Louis objected so much to the idea of paying a fair share to the République, he just hadn't figured out a way to explain the source of his income.

Louis, Marguerite and Mama all lived - not in luxury by any means - but not wanting too much either in the way

101

of necessities. The old madam seemed happy and never gave any hint that anything was amiss, blissfully anticipating her weekly jaunts into the countryside with Marguerite at the wheel of the old colonel's Daimler.

But Louis had never been able to completely shake off the memories of his time in Marseille, so occasionally a worry would worm its way into his thoughts, a prickly little thorn that irritated his contentment and – a little less often now - his conscience. But that was only because he had developed a little fondness for the old madam.

Whenever he would look at the list in preparation for a trip to Aix, he'd see just how far down it he had gotten and worry a bit more, afraid that one day Madam would suddenly realize that so many things had gone missing from the chateau.

 One day after Marguerite had loaded the madam in the car and left for the countryside, Louis realized that he couldn't go on as he had been. He needed to say something to Mama about his concerns. He explained to her that there was nothing wrong in particular, he just worried that too much of a good thing might be their undoing. Just being careful, like she had taught him. He certainly didn't want to leave her again. He didn't want to leave Marguerite. He *really* didn't want to go back to Marseille again.

Mama just smiled. Something was obviously stirring around in that sharp old mind of hers, and when she said nothing, Louis was afraid that she had missed the point he was trying to make. He began again to express his concerns when Mama held up a skinny little finger to her lips. He stopped in mid-sentence and waited.

That was the day that Mama had told him her little secret.

"When Marguerite first came to the chateau and began driving Madam around the countryside, I had a lot of time to look around this big old house", she said. "I was finally able to figure out some answers to a lot of questions I had. Where did the old couple come from? Why was the house so fancy inside where only they could see how well-off they were. Anyone in the village would see nothing but the worn-out and crumbling building from the outside, like a couple of poor farmers lived there – squatters in a fallen down mansion. Normal people just weren't like that. They liked to show off their wealth to the world, not hide it away."

Mama caught her breath and looked at Louis. She was

amused by the look on his face. The raised eyebrows, the pursed lips, told her he was steeling himself for another episode of her lively imagination, perhaps even then remembering some of the stories she had written to him at Marseille – expecting just another of her wild ramblings.

She smiled to herself for she admitted to having an imagination that often ventured outside the bounds of believability. But oddly, that had helped keep her sane in the darker days of an often grey life. But this time there was a difference. She had to finish this particular story and then she'd see if he believed, if he really understood what she was telling him.

"And then there was their strange accents," she continued and shook her head as if to clear the sound of them from her ears. "You know I've never been further away from Aix than to Arles or Avignon, so I just thought they talked like someone up north would, maybe from Paris or Strasberg. And occasionally, some curious sounding word would come tumbling out of her mouth when she would get upset. They were words I didn't know and I would pretend I hadn't heard them. The old madam would get a strange expression on her face that looked like she wanted to gobble up those words and hoped nobody had noticed."

Mama looked lost in her own thoughts for a moment and then turning back to Louis said, "Something kept bothering me about it, though. It was not just the accent but a hundred little things. Nothing by itself meant much but everything together gave me an itch I just had to scratch," she laughed. "I just couldn't let it go without knowing. So whenever I had some time to myself at the chateau, I'd keep looking around.

A little while after the old monsieur died, Madam had me moving things out of his closet and putting them down in the cellar. I think she was looking for something but she never said so."

"In the very back of his closet there was a big old wooden trunk that looked like it had been through some very rough times. It took both me and Marguerite to drag it to the cellar. The next time Marguerite took her out driving, I went back down to the cellar and opened the trunk. Not much there. It had been so heavy carrying it down from the bedroom that I hoped it was full of valuables, maybe more silver or nice china from up at Limoge. But it was just paper – hundreds of old letters and such. I didn't read any of them then, but there were some strange markings on them that I couldn't get out of my mind. They sure looked familiar but I couldn't remember at all where I had seen them. I took a few of the letters next time I went to Aix and visited the library."

"Every time I'd go to Aix to mail a letter to you, Louis, I'd go to the library. I couldn't believe how much I was learning." With a twinkle in her eyes that Louis didn't miss, she said, "And I couldn't believe *what* I was learning. It was finally dawning on this old woman how much I'd missed by not getting more education when I was young. But alas" she sighed, "Youth was a time for work and families, not going to school and spending time at libraries."

Louis was amazed at the excitement in Mama's voice. He knew she had quite a strong imagination but he also knew she had a sharp mind. He hadn't paid that much attention when he was younger, but since coming home from Marseille, she had often surprised him with her wit and cunning. She had a gift for thinking through a problem and finding the right answer.

"This may really surprise you," she said with a sly grin, "but I'm getting to know a little bit about art, especially about our own Cezanne. His work is wonderful, you know. I didn't realize that Provence was so beautiful until I looked at Cezanne's paintings. And I didn't know

106

his art was so wonderful until I really started to look at Provence." She smiled at her turn of words.

"Every time I'd look at his pictures in books at the library, I'd see a real life version of it on the way back home. You can see his mountain from the chateau and I'd come home and just sit and look at it. That's how I was so sure that the picture hanging on Madam's bedroom wall was really one of his. It just spoke to me and made me feel good even when things weren't always so good."

"I don't think she liked it in that same way. If she did she never said anything." Mama seemed to stop for another breath and looked at Louis as if she had just realized a great truth, "Art needs to be loved and enjoyed," she said with a conviction that surprised Louis.

"That's when I started to think about that painting in another way. To Madam it just seemed another picture – any old picture – to decorate a wall with. She never seemed to pay any attention to it, never just stop and look at it or run her finger across the brush marks. But I had come to love it. I could stand and look at it and feel like I was floating on a cloud over the real scene – a very lucky person given a very special privilege.

It was a thing of so much beauty, but what it represented was even more beautiful. The more I thought about it the more beautiful it became, and what it could mean became more important than its beauty.   But I knew my idea would have to wait until you came home."

Louis had listened to her saga like the dutiful son that he was, but he still didn't understand. Mama was a good storyteller, but she hadn't given him a reason not to worry. Perhaps she was just avoiding the question. Or perhaps – sadly – just becoming a poor old fool full of fantasies. He steadied himself and decided that he'd hear her out.   Patience was a trait that he had honed to a fine edge in Marseille.

She went on with her strange story. "The biggest mystery to me - among so many at the old chateau - were the paintings, the ones in madam's bedroom. If they were real, they could be worth a huge fortune. There was the Cezanne, a little picture by Piccasso, another one by Dufy and a pretty one by Pissaro that had been torn and then repaired by sewing it back together. Because of my idea for the Cezanne and everything I'd learned at the library and the museums, it occurred to me that I ought to find out what was in the heavy wooden crates hidden at the very back of the

108

old cellar. Every time Madam and Marguerite went driving I'd open one of the crates," she stopped and swallowed hard as if the mere contemplation of her discovery made the words hard to mouth, " and then I'd carefully put everything back just as I'd found it."

"Louis," she said, taking one of his hands between her own, "What I found was at least a dozen beautiful paintings hidden in these heavy wooden boxes, dozing peacefully in that cellar. You might not know the names but I've seen them in the books," and she added, "I think they're real."

"But more important, I found the answer to the second biggest mystery at the chateau." She looked straight into his eyes to make sure he was following her reasoning. "How could ordinary people have pieces of art like those. Precious art on your bedroom walls that no one could see and appreciate; beautiful paintings hidden away in your cellar in rough wooden boxes, just waiting to be eaten by rats or rot under a slime of mold."

"The papers that I found in that battered old trunk in the back of Le Monsieur's closet - and digging into the library's history books – gave me the answer." Mama stopped and took a deep breath. She sensed that Louis was finally ready to know what she knew.

"The old monsieur," she said to him, "wasn't from Paris or Strasberg or even France. I guess I've told you a lot of wild stories that you didn't believe. I realize that now. But believe what I'm telling you now. I can show you the papers. I know who he is without a doubt." Mama had a good flair for the dramatic. She waited to tantalize Louis a bit and to make sure he was listening.

Louis was listening – intently.

She took up her story again, "His name was Manfred Halmeyer . . . . Colonel Manfred Halmeyer. He was an assistant of some kind to that old Nazi General Hermann Goering." She let that sink in to see if Louis understood the importance of what she was telling him. He did. His jaw had dropped in astonishment. She continued.

"Near the end of the big war, the Colonel had been transferred out of Germany and was stationed in Vichy. I think he was sent down to help keep tabs on the occupation government, making sure they weren't going to turn on the Nazis. Lot of good that did," she spat out, "He was a thief and crook like his boss. In fact, he stole some of the art from Goering that Goering had stolen from the Jews. The old Colonel was probably glad to put some distance between himself and Goering in case his boss ever found out.

Instead of running off to South America after the war, the Colonel, with the help of some friends in Vichy, quietly came to Provence and moved into the old abandoned chateau. He and Madam lived a quiet life, barely leaving the place, for fear of discovery - living off stolen art. Apparently, the Colonel hadn't done anything that made him a target for the Allies to hunt down. He just lived quietly and stayed out of sight. "

"Do you remember," she asked Louis, "when I wrote you that he had died; that a big car had come and quietly taken his body away. I now know that Madam made the arrangements for that to happen. It wasn't a service that could be trusted to a local undertaker. It seems there's a secret network of old Nazis and their sympathizers that cleans up such dirty leftovers of the war years."

"After living barricaded for so long in the big house, Madam actually felt safer after the Colonel was gone. After all she wasn't the Nazi. It would be ok to get out some. I think I helped her see that, and then Marguerite came." Mama finished and looked at Louis.

His jaw had clamped shut and there was the beginning of a smile. He understood – perfectly.

She laid out the final chapter of her plan. Marguerite could continue to drive Madam in the countryside and Louis could continue to make his visits to Aix. They wouldn't have to worry about Madam suddenly realizing that many things were missing from the house.

Who would she tell? How could she explain a hundred things? Was she going to tell the police that these Frenchmen were selling off the valuables that her Nazi husband and his boss Goering had stolen from the rest of Europe? Mama knew that wasn't a problem. Mama had thought also about the art. Taking one of those now just might be too much for the old lady to ignore even if ignoring it was in her best interest. But the old lady was becoming ancient, couldn't last very much longer.

As soon as she dropped, they would whisk the art out of the chateau to an already prepared hiding place. Thrice stolen art! What irory! Their plan now required only that they wait. In the meantime the old chateau still held a wealth of looted – and salable – goods.

Louis agreed and was much relieved by Mama's

revelation, but still there was something he had to tell her. A problem had been nagging at him for some time but he hesitated to be the bearer of bad news. Mama wasn't young anymore and any threat to her cherished plan might be too much for her to bear. But he had to tell someone and if he couldn't tell Mama, then who?

As Louis now sat in the quiet of the bastide, he thought back to that very day when he had stood looking out a window of the old Chateau, listening to Mama's fantastic story. He remembered the glint of sunlight off the distant car . . . Marguerite taking the old Madam off into the countryside for one of the rambling afternoons she loved so well. They'd be gone for hours.

After hearing her fantastic story and seeing the look of excitement transform her old face, he had turned his back to Mama. He didn't want to see her face when he disclosed his own secret. A secret that would instantly wreck the plan she had laid out with so much relish. Her anguished and disappointed face had haunted his dreams too many times; he couldn't look at her now. He stood with both hands on the stone window sill as if propping up his courage and fixed his gaze on the distant speck of light, shrinking into nothing much like Mama's plan would after he confessed his own terrible secret.

113

"Mama, when I said there was nothing wrong . . . . well, I meant to tell you. . ." he hesitated, waiting for a sound.

 She said nothing.

 Louis continued, "You remember when I took the large silver tray with the gold edging to Aix. We hoped that such a valuable piece would bring a price that could get us ahead. Maybe get another doctor to look at Jo's leg." He didn't want to look at Mama when he mentioned Jo either. He could feel Mama's look of displeasure burning on his back. He quickly changed the subject from one he wished he hadn't brought up to the one he wished he didn't have to reveal now.

"It didn't bring as much as we hoped." He waited for some sign that she was listening . . . a movement, a sigh. Still nothing.

He stayed at the window and went on, "It did bring a good price, a very good price, but there was a problem." Unable to staunch the flood now, "there was a policemen. I couldn't have known, he was in regular clothes, not a uniform. He seemed to be waiting. When I had sold the silver and took payment , he came from nowhere, grabbed me by the arm and shoved a badge in my face. Mama, the square at Aix all of a sudden looked just like the prison yard at Marseille." The very name was a fishbone in his throat. He couldn't bear to turn now, so he plowed on.

"He wanted part of the money. I had to give him half to keep him from arresting me. I don't think I can go back to Aix anymore. I'll have to find another market and just hope I have the nerve left." There, he'd said it. And it had had to be said. In a way, he was relieved even if now he would have to deal with the consequences. He turned back from the window to measure the damage – to see the look of disappointment and despair on Mama's old face – to see what the destruction of her hopes had done to her.

When he turned and saw her face, her look wasn't what he had expected; it was simply worse.

She was smiling.

She either hadn't understood a word, or if she had, the news had had a devastating effect. It had shocked her right out of reality. Louis crossed the room and knelt in front of her. He took her old hands in his and began to sooth her. When she spoke, the strength of her voice surprised him.

"Shhh,' she hissed through her smile. She laid a thin
hand along his cheek and said, "of course, you're going
back to Aix and here's what you're going to do." She
explained what he was to do and Louis' load lifted like a
last minute reprieve at the gallows. She had heard
every word. Mama, it seemed, was full of surprises.

Chapter Twelve

On Louis' next trip to Aix, he took the largest, most
valuable piece from the Chateau's inventory that he
dared. He also took Jo. He felt sure the large, silver
candelabra would attract the policeman's attention,
especially if Louis diligently searched the crowds for the
right face before making his move. He had all the time
in the world. The cop was there alright and was on
Louis at the first glint of silver. Louis quietly took
payment for the beautiful piece and as quietly paid the
policeman an obscene amount to avoid arrest. Then he
and Jo went home and related their experience to
Mama.

The following week Louis was back in Aix searching the
crowds for the now familiar face. He waited and grew
tired carrying the largest piece he had ever brought to
Aix – a small bronze statue of St. Jude, the patron saint
of lost causes. The irony of his selection had appealed
to Louis until he had carried the heavy thing around for
close to three hours. Where were the police when you
needed them, he thought wryly to himself. Giving up
on seeing the policeman, he decided to approach the
one of his usual buyers who was most likely to want the

piece, take his money and go home.   Gratefully, Louis had read his buyer correctly, for he not only was interested in the statue but paid a handsome sum for it – more than Louis expected.

Louis thanked him and turned to go and walked straight into the policeman. By now the routine demanded that both quietly step to a private place to finish their affairs. Louis followed the policeman to a side street and into a secluded doorway. He slowly counted out half the value of the little bronze saint and reaching into his pocket, took out a piece of paper that he added to the price of his continued freedom and laid both in the policeman's outstretched hand. Louis smiled and said thank you, a response that the policeman thought quite peculiar.

The policeman looked at the bulky amount of currency in his hand and saw the paper that Louis had placed on the top. The policeman's countenance froze and the blood drained from his face. He looked quite pale, as if a ghost somehow perched atop the bundle of Euros

 The paper on top of the stack of notes was a very clear picture of him accepting Euros from Louis, a felon of record, who oddly was looking full face at the camera and smiling. The policeman's own internal guilt was

118

now compounded by photographic proof of his guilt. The thief simply stood there and said nothing, but his demeanor could be translated as "you can keep this picture, I have other copies."

The policeman already hated himself for taking money from this man, and now he hated himself even more for the fear that he felt. The only redeeming thing the policeman could think of in his defense was his reason for what he had done. The money was not for himself. It was for his wife and his daughters, for his old mother. There had been so much illness in his family and it broke his heart when he was unable to get them help. Doctors were expensive.

In spite of what he had done, he knew that he was still a good cop. Even good people could make mistakes. But now he was at the mercy of this man standing in front of him, not taunting, but clearly waiting for a response. The policeman wasn't the kind of man who had a ready answer for this situation. It was new to him. He was simply dumbstruck.

He knew what he *should* do. He should arrest this thief and suffer the consequences for what he had done; that was the kind of man, the kind of policeman he was. The thought kept playing in his head like a scratched record while he stood toe to toe with the man who smiled at him. No obvious answer came.

What would happen to him and his family when he had no job, he might even lose his freedom for what he had done. He knew for certain that Soutier would have his badge. His superior had taken every possible opportunity to criticize him, and especially loved to berate him in front of his deputy, a snarling little brute that seemed to enjoy the policeman's embarrassment.

To the policeman, there was little doubt that his superior actually enjoyed it also and he knew exactly why – a reason he couldn't and wouldn't argue with. The policeman had won many commendations for his successful work on the streets. With each commendation, it was a reminder that the policeman was the better cop and that he, the superior had not a single thing to recommend him, and that his job was the result - not of astute detective work – but of family connections.

The policeman was at a loss. What were his present choices? He absurdly looked at the other man as if he might have the answer. But the other man simply stood there, waiting, perhaps expecting to be arrested, perhaps . . .

The policeman had to do something, he had to make a decision. That day Louis and Maurice DesVaux, the policeman, became friends.

Having carried the heavy statue around the market all morning, Louis had developed an appetite that was born not only from more exertion than he was accustomed to but also from the pleasure of seeing a plan succeed. Louis invited the policeman to lunch at a tiny Viet Namese restaurant in a back alley behind the square. Maurice DesVaux accepted, almost meekly, and followed Louis to lunch.

They shared a carafe of the local red, Coteau d'Aix, before another word was spoken. Louis was working up his courage to speak and the policeman, still in shock, waited for the other shoe to fall.

Finally, Maurice DesVaux, policeman, could stand the strain no longer. "Monsieur," he began, as he pushed his hand across the table, "I am a good policeman. Here is your money back. I don't know why I did this." He hesitated as if searching inside himself, and finding an answer, said, "Well, yes, I do know. I needed the money. I have a wife, three little children and an old mother who is ill. They all depend on me to fill their stomachs and cloth their backs and put a roof over their

121

heads. And to make them well when they fall ill. Please take the money back. And I beg of you, let's keep this quiet. You seem like a decent man and I have so many who depend on me."

Louis could not understand about the children although he wished that he could. He did understand about the responsibilities for an old mother. Maybe even a wife. He pushed the money back across the table, feeling a small bit of sympathy for the man who sat opposite. The man who no longer felt like a threat, a man who looked like a normal person with normal problems, Louis' kind of problems.

Louis and Maurice talked quietly through a long Provencal lunch. Maurice felt strained and uncomfortable, but as all wise men can bear witness, good food and generous portions of red wine promote good conversation and foster affable feelings even between adversaries.

Maurice finally allowed himself to talk about his family and his work as a policeman. Louis also talked about his mother but left Marseille for another time. When it came time for coffee, Louis was feeling that he could safely move to the next stage of the conversation and suggested that they retire to another, even quieter café down the alley for an aperitif.

By the time they had worked their way perilously near the bottom of a bottle of pastis, Louis had laid out most of the bare bones of his story. Maurice listened with a stoic expression until Louis had finished.

"Monsieur Jaubert, why are you telling me about all this. I have apologized for my errors and wish I could give back what I have already taken from you. Unfortunately, I do not have it any longer. All that I have left is a small amount of dignity and I have stupidly risked that for a few Euros." Maurice was worried that a pleasant lunch was now turning into a shakedown. "What do you want from me?"

Louis hurried to the part where Maurice was to be included in his plan. Maurice stiffened, "Monsieur, I feel badly enough taking money from you, but you're a . . . . " he lowered his eyes and cleared his throat. "But to steal from regular people, I couldn't, I am still a policeman." Maurice hoped that he meant it. He wasn't especially feeling like it at the moment.

Louis had saved his closing argument just in the event that the policeman was still unconvinced. He told

Maurice about Colonel Manfred Halmeyer and how he had stolen from General Hermann Goering who had stolen from Europe's Jews. About Halmeyer who had slipped away from the Allies and hidden in Provence right under their noses and had the audacity to live leisurely and unpunished off the proceeds of his ill gotten gains. The old Nazi had gone on to whatever awaited him in the hereafter and the old madam was sure to follow shortly.

Louis had come to see his activities as a kind of justice for those who had had everything taken away from them and a retribution and punishment for the Nazis who thoroughly deserved both. And of course, Louis added, he'd never ever consider doing such things only for himself.

But he too had a wife and an old mother who deserved an easier time in her older years. And of course, he quickly added, if he had children to feed and care for, he would do anything for them. Louis stopped talking and took a slow drink of his pastis, waiting.

"Monsieur," Maurice said with gravity, "I don't agree with what you do, but perhaps now I am beginning to understand some of your reasons." The wine, the pastis and a truly likable and persuasive Louis had put the

124

policeman more at ease. Relieved that he wasn't being blackmailed, he no longer worried so much about Soutier and his ridiculous little shadow, Poulenc. Now all he had to worry about was his own conscience.

Maurice swirled the last bit of pastis in his glass while he thought about what to say. Maybe he was being selfish and was worrying too much about himself and his reputation. A man's pride could be his undoing. Justice was a policeman's work and if he had a chance to see some justice done in the world why would it be so bad if his family happened to see a little benefit as a result.

Especially, the chance to see justice done. After all, that was what had won him his citations. That was what being a policeman was all about.

However, something still nagged at his conscience.

"What I do not understand, Monsieur Jaubert," . . . .

"Please call me Louis," Louis interrupted

"What I do not understand, Louis, is why you *want* to include me in your, ah, activities." Maurice said. The policeman himself wasn't sure whether he had just stated an objection or made a request for more information.

Louis, sensing a chance to close the sale, took another swallow of pastis and finished spelling out the role he envisioned for Maurice along with the substantial benefits.

Maurice was beginning to grasp the finer points of Louis' plan. If some personal benefit happened to result from trying to correct a grave injustice, sometimes that's just how things worked out. Surely a policeman could never reject justice out-of-hand for any reason.

Maybe he'd been too quick in rushing to judgment; maybe he had, in fact, underestimated this man. The more he thought about it the more sense it made, and the more sense it made the more he could understand Louis' point of view. Not only was Louis' argument beginning to sound logical, one could respect even a thief who was so considerate of his old mother. Not to mention his handicapped nephew. And of course revenge or amends or justice - whatever one called it - against the despicable Nazis was not an unworthy objective.

Of course, Louis hadn't explained how his plans for the

126

Cezanne that hung on the back wall of the old madam's boudoir might exact any meaningful revenge on the old departed Nazi, and Maurice simply hadn't thought to ask.

A battle had been waged deep in the policeman's soul. His demon persuading in one ear and his angel pleading in the other – pushing and pulling the policeman in a tug-of-war that bruised both nerves and conscience.

Not unexpectedly, in this kind of struggle, a winner often emerges too quickly and what later stood as the singular disappointment to the policeman with himself, was the fact that he could not clearly give name to the winner. But while he thought of his choices and matched them with the consequences, he thought of his family.

Moments passed, and almost without his realizing it, a decision came upon him like a shadow. It came fully formed and without further need of his deliberation. Maurice slowly raised his glass and looked at Louis. "To justice," he said quietly, his voice almost a whisper. His attention dropped to the stack of Euros still on the table in front of him.

Louis eyed the cash too and saw that the picture Jo had

127

taken of him and Maurice still lay atop the Euros. Louis liked this man. He picked up the photograph, studied it for a moment and raised his gaze to the face of the man across the table. He noticed a faint tick pull at the corner of the policeman's mouth. Louis also observed the tight lines around the policeman's eyes relax ever so slightly when he crumpled the picture in his big hand and tossed it into a nearby trash can.

"Maurice," Louis said, "I have to ask you a question. The first time we met . . . how did you know it wasn't my piece of silver to sell?"

Maurice shrugged his shoulders and gave Louis a thin smile, "You looked guilty" he said . . . "and you paid too fast."

Louis didn't laugh, but he did manage a weak smile.

Louis and Maurice met for lunch and transacted their business each week, and waited. Their friendship grew as they talked of many things. Louis Jaubert came to understand how a man can give over his life to the law and even be willing to sacrifice himself for its ideals –

some of which the man may not always possess and treasure as his own.   Maurice DesVaux began to see how a man could bend - even break - the law without malice and without repudiating all his honor and dignity.

 As their friendship grew, both men came to believe that no one is all good or all bad but that all men walk a very narrow path where obstacles and booby traps can easily send a man sprawling on either side.   Each man simply accepted the others flaws and valued his virtues and enjoyed their uncommon camaraderie.

Within a year of Mama's revealing her secret to Louis, the old madam drifted away in her sleep. Louis had made the necessary arrangements with the local undertaker called in to remove the madam to her final resting place. No need now for special precautions. Mama, Louis, and Marguerite – now Louis' wife- retreated back to the cottage to consider their next step. And the old chateau began another period of decline.

Both Louis and Mama Jaubert had been surprised when tears had unexpectedly trickled down their own faces at the old madams interment. Perhaps the tears were for the old madam and perhaps one or two were for the old chateau, soon to be in death throes of its own.

Chapter Thirteen

Louis paced about the old bastide and thought about their plan, and waited. He had waited for over two years to make sure the next step was the right one; that they had considered all the risks. He had even picked up on mama's habit of visiting libraries and museums and learning all he could about art.

They had put so much work into their plan. Then marguerite had walked out. At first Louis had feared she would talk and ruin everything, but Mama had said absolutely not; there was nothing to worry about. Marguerite was too involved to say a word. After all, it was she who had diverted the old lady with the long drives in the country. She had also enjoyed the benefits of Louis' visits to Aix, and needless to say, she would expect something when the plan paid off.

But Marguerite was still gone, Louis thought, and now what was supposed to be the easy finish to their plan was blowing up in his face. He still didn't know what to make of the last call from Paulo. The American was a big puzzle. He always seemed to be in the wrong place at the wrong time. It hadn't been that difficult for Paulo to find them in Aix. A few calls to the biggest tourist hotels and Paulo had found them on the fourth call – at Le Hotel Cezanne. Paulo had thought the irony of it very funny.

He had followed them through the rainy streets of Aix to the Musee Brabet . Paulo had taken a table by the window in a café across the street and waited. He waited and drank expresso for over an hour. Finally the big doors of the museum opened and the American with his wife and daughter came out into the rain.

Paulo pushed his expresso cup aside and started to stand up, ready to follow, when a police van pulled up to the curb in front of the museum. Paulo, always alert to any police activity, sat back down. He then saw two policemen come out of the building just behind the Americans. They seemed to be directing the family toward the van.

 To Paulo's surprise, the van doors flew open and the Americans were roughly herded in.   The policemen quickly surveyed the rain-swept street up and down, and climbed in behind them. The van sped away, throwing a torrent on a hapless passerby.

 Louis was starting to feel sorry for the American. His

luck was just as bad as Louis', maybe even worse. He was sure the poor guy had never expected his vacation to take the turns that it had.

Louis thought about the positives. It was good to work with someone like Paulo. Paulo was smart and knew what to do in every situation. After the Americans were taken away, Paulo had hurried back to their hotel . He let himself into their room, searched it thoroughly and carefully but found neither tube nor canvas. He did find the Americans wallet. He took just enough to cover the days expenses. Louis chuckled when he thought about Paulo's sense of propriety.

 It was now evident that the American had taken his painting to the museum, probably to ask their assistance somehow. It was equally evident that his painting, just like the American family, was now in the custody of the Aix police.

Louis smiled. Strangely enough, perhaps things were finally turning in his favor. He picked up his cell phone and dialed a number he knew by heart.

Maurice DesVaux answered on the third ring.

Chapter Fourteen

Diane, Beth and Sam were told to sit along a hard metal bench on one side of the van. The two policemen sat directly across with the same menacing look they brought from the museum director's office. The uniformed officer still rested his hand on his sidearm. Sam thought it a good way to keep down dissent and wasn't about to resist at this point. Beth was sobbing, Diane was seething and Sam was wondering what the hell was going on.

The van ran carelessly through the rain slick streets and Sam was afraid they'd not survive the trip to wherever they were being taken. They made it somehow and pulled to a stop in a narrow alley behind a police station. The cops motioned them back out into the rain, which had picked up in intensity. By the time they ran the few steps to the station entrance, splashing through deep puddles, they were totally soaked.

If the museum director's office had been stark and cold, the police station by comparison was several rungs down the ladder. The sparse furniture was old and dilapidated but fit in perfectly well with the grey and grimy walls, walls that had been witness to the end-of-the-line processing of countless criminals. The walls seemed to close in on the Bakers and scream of their guilt. They were advised to be cooperative. The police gave the impression that they blamed Sam and his family for the fact that they too were soaked.

Still in their soggy clothes, they were escorted into an empty room. Empty, except for three chairs along the front of a plain wooden desk with another chair facing them on the opposite side; the placement of the dingy furniture in the cheerless room gave promise of more unpleasantness to come.

They sat stunned.

"Don't you think we should call the U.S. embassy," Diane asked.

"Great plan, Mom," Beth was near to tears again, "But they took our cell phones."

"They've got to give us our one call, right?" Sam asked Diane. He was shaking with anger but hadn't wanted to complicate their situation by grabbing that rude little policeman who loved to play with his gun and shaking some sense into him. Not only had they insulted him and his family, they had endangered their very lives with their wild ride through the slick streets of the city. Sam was sure that Diane and Beth would have bruises from being bounced around the rough van and he expected that his old bruises from Avignon might develop some new ones of their own.

"Do you still think we did this the right way," Diane began.

"Don't, Mom," Beth sobbed.

"But there's something crazy going on here," Diane continued.

"It's got to be some kind of misunderstanding," Sam Said, "Maybe with my bad French I said something the wrong way. They can't actually think we tried to steal anything, can they?" At that moment, sitting in wet, chilly clothes, on hard chairs in a grey room, Sam wasn't so sure about that. They waited uneasily.

Diane and Beth fell into fitful sleep. Sam stewed and wondered what was taking so long for someone to come to their senses and let them go.

The gloomy daylight turned to dusk and the small

window high up on the one wall gave them their only light. Sam's stomach was beginning to rumble and so was his head. He wished that someone would come in even if it meant unpleasantness.

The incessant drumming of the rain on a metal roof just outside the room was beginning to remind Sam of torture methods he'd read about. Diane and Beth still dozed, holding each other, and Sam sat trying his best to figure out how their vacation had taken such a wrong turn. Maybe someday this would be a great story but at this moment it was a nightmare.

The room's only door flew open and banged into the wall, making the room reverberate like a bass drum. The sharpness of it startled all three of them from their stupor. The officers who brought them from the Brabet were now accompanied by another man, this one not in uniform. His shiny black suit flecked with cigarette ashes on both lapels. The jacket and trousers, while close in shade, didn't match and hung haphazardly about his gaunt form. The once white shirt was so oversized at the neck that it gave him a turtle like appearance. He sat at the desk across from them.

The uniformed officer stood at his back, his hand still

resting on top of his gun. His mouth seemed frozen in a permanent sneer, and through nicotine stained teeth hissed an introduction, "Monsieur, this is Inspector Soutier. It will be best to cooperate with him."

When the man at the desk opened his mouth, the turtle-like gentility disappeared. His sharp features took on the look of a carnivore climbing out of its den and about to spring on its prey. He started to address them in very rapid French. Between the speed of his speech and an accent that Sam had never heard before, he understood nothing the man said.

A confused look on Sam's face must have communicated his incomprehension. The man abruptly stopped, "And I suppose you expect me to speak your language?" He made it sound thoroughly distasteful.

If you want an answer, Sam thought. "Yes," Sam said.

"I must see your identification papers," the inspector said. Sam had forgotten his wallet again, so Diane and Beth who both had their passports with them had to vouch for the family's identity.

Mr. Baker, You are in a great deal of trouble. Why do you feel that you can come to our country and steal the

138

patrimoine of France and walk freely away?

"I haven't stolen anything," Sam protested.

He shook a finger at Sam, indicating that he would tolerate no argument.

Diane took the opportunity to demand that they be allowed to call their embassy.

He sneered again, bigger, showing his own tobacco yellowed teeth, "And why do you think your embassy would be interested in helping art thieves."

It was too much. "We're not art thieves," Sam said.

The finger wagged again, but Sam went on, "we were just enjoying a simple vacation when this painting was dumped in my lap – literally."

"Tell me what you mean," the man said, as he pulled a rumpled pack of cigarettes from the side pocket of his jacket. He looked at the cigarettes through narrowed eyes as if trying to decide whether he really wanted to smoke. He finally hung one from his lower lip, struck a match on the desk, lit up, and threw the match on the floor. He took a long pull from the cigarette and then slowly and deliberately blew the smoke in their direction. He leaned over on the desk with his rheumy eyes bearing down on Diane and said again, "Tell me what you mean." Diane felt uncomfortable at the man's stare and diverted her eyes to Sam.

He's finally listening, Sam thought and told him the same story that he had told the museum director, including the part in Avignon.

He man laughed, "And you insult me, monsieur, expecting me to believe such an incredible story. You simply make your problem worse." He abruptly got up and started out of the room. Sam got up too, but the uniformed man took a step forward, hand back on his gun. Diane put her hand on Sam's arm, "Don't Sam, it's ok."

The black suit turned back and delivered the bleak news, "Monsieur, you are in for a long stay in France. A a very long stay." Then appearing to find some extra satisfaction in the thought, he added, "but not a very pleasant one."

 He was gone and the uniformed man went out right behind him. They heard a lock click into place as the door slammed shut.

Chapter Fifteen

A sharp rap came at the big metal door of the museum director's office. The hollow echo startled the director causing him to jump up from his desk, "Entrée," he called out. The door swung open. Inspector Soutier and officer Poulenc came in. Soutier turned and locked the door. He had a self-satisfied smugness showing through the harsh features of his face. The director despised this hateful man but business was business and he could endure his haughtiness for a few more days and then he was out of this lousy office and this third rate museum.

On the other hand, he thoroughly hated Soutier's stupid shadow, Poulenc. Soutier called him his assistant - what a joke! The little rat faced flic would probably ruin the whole thing if Soutier didn't rein him in and make him keep his mouth shut. The little braggart had given them more than one scare by boasting about 'their' business and his close association with the Inspector.

Soutier sat down hard in one of the cheap chairs and stretched out his gangly legs, propping his booted feet on the Director's desk. He didn't like the arrogant director and didn't care whether he liked his boots on his desk or not. He actually felt pleased when a red flush of anger rose in the director's cheeks. He was tired of playing salesman when the director decided that some item from the museum's collection had become superfluous, and could be quietly disposed of. But he knew they both needed the money. Still it was a lot of risk for small returns.

In spite of Soutier's loathing for the pompous little bureaucrat, he had to give the director credit on this one. When the American had walked into the director's office and literally dropped a gift from heaven in their laps, he recognized the opportunity for riches that would free them from their pedantic lives forever.

And they'd never have to deal with each other again. That was almost as important as the money.

The director had called him immediately and laid out his quickly hatched scheme. He, the director – since an item of such obvious value required the skills and knowledge of a professional – would find a buyer if Soutier could convince the American to forget he had ever seen the painting. The American and his family had to be frightened so thoroughly that they would never think of mentioning the painting to anyone.

Maybe that wasn't absolutely necessary, he thought, but at least Soutier agreed with him on this. They wanted no one asking any questions until they were well out of the country. A little fear and intimidation should work nicely since he knew Soutier to be adept at such arts.

Soutier wasn't sure if he should be pleased or insulted by the remarks. That was a laugh, he thought, the director calling himself a 'professional'. He wouldn't know how to find a buyer and both jobs would fall to himself. In the end, he'd have to share after having done all the work and taking all the risks. But if he could make it work, it would be worth it.

Intimidation, he could do. He had done. The American and his family were frightened to the point of thinking they were headed straight to Devil's Island. He had enjoyed watching the American sweat. The arrogant and superior feeling Americans could be scared just like anybody else. And Poulenc hadn't had as much fun in years.

He wondered to himself if the director had done his

part of the bargain, after all it was a new role for him. It had always been Soutier who - with numerous contacts and long experience in the darker side of Provence - had found the buyers and negotiated the sales. But since it had fallen to him to take care of the American, the Director now would have to find a buyer, and quickly.

While the director was letting the blood drain out of his face, Soutier decided to begin. "We've got the American and his family so scared that they are ready to get out of France and forget the painting – forget they ever saw it. Probably forget they've ever been to France" Soutier laughed coarsely.

He was pleased that his skills still held a sharp edge. He thought how amusing and satisfying it would be to apply his 'arts' to the director. Maybe after it was all over, he'd allow himself this one little pleasure. Who could the director complain to? That thought made the prospect all the more appealing. A smile escaped his lips that he felt sure the director must have noticed.

"And you have found a buyer, non? Soutier pushed, knowing the answer.

The director could feel the condescending gaze boring

into him. "Not yet, but I have made some important calls." He took a thin folder from the top drawer and put it in front of himself as if it were proof that had a buyer imminent. He held it close in case the Inspector should reach for it. They both knew it was empty.

Poulenc saw the chance to be useful. "There is a Russian sniffing around looking for art to buy," he smiled at his own audacity, showing nicotine teeth again.

Both the Director and Soutier stiffened at Poulenc's remarks.

"Where did you hear this?" Soutier turned sharply on him.

"I heard DesVaux talking to someone on the phone at the station. Probably one of his petty little informers. Said he'd bet that it was the same Russian who had been trying to buy the painting before it got dumped in the American's lap by mistake."

Poulenc's rambling hit Soutier like a bullet. How could Desvaux know about the painting? How did he know it was on the market – the only important Cezanne that Provence had seen in decades being chased by foreign money. Money that he intended to put in his pocket.

DesVaux had always been a pain in the arse. He was always rounding up some petty criminal before Soutier could get to them. It was embarrassing. After all, Soutier was his superior and DesVaux didn't have the good grace to pass on a little credit when he could.

Now that would change.

The Director saw the chance for his own rescue, "What's he talking about, Soutier? Is this possible?"

Soutier was thinking fast. It didn't feel quite right but he wasn't about to let DesVaux beat him out this time. Not on something this big. Not on something that could mean a plush retirement. He'd have to move fast but he couldn't put pressure on DesVaux himself. The little cop could play tough, he knew that from experience.

"Yes," he said more confidently than he felt. "I'll have Poulenc question him about it. But we'll have to move fast before the American regains his nerve."

The mention of the interrogation of the American family was more than Poulenc could resist. In telling the Director, he could enjoy it all again, "The girl was crying, the woman was wringing her hands," Poulenc smirked as if his fierce rat face was solely responsible, "and every time the man started to say anything, I'd let my hand slide down to my pistol. Then the man would shut up and sit down. It was so funny . . . he almost. . ."

"Shut up, Poulenc." Soutier cut him off and lifted his feet from the desk and leaned forward in the too-small chair, his black eyes blazing at the Director, "They will never say a thing. When we let them go, they will be out of France quicker than it takes a Parisien to . . .

"What do you mean, 'when you let them go'? You still have them in custody? Where are they? Have they called their embassy?"

"They are under 'house arrest' at their hotel." Soutier said. "And No, they haven't contacted their embassy." He tried to sound especially sinister for the Director's benefit, "I convinced them that it would be a very bad idea." He didn't like being interrupted and particularly didn't like the tone of the director's question.

"Isn't that dangerous? Why didn't you keep them at the station? What if someone at the hotel interferes?" The Director was getting agitated, "How long do you plan to keep them?"

Soutier shot to his feet, "Shut up, Fourcere, I'll take care of my part. Just what have you done?" His eyes bored in on the folder in front of the director. He thought about grabbing it off the desk just to show the smug director that he knew it was empty but what was the point?

It was the first time Soutier had called the Director by his name instead of his title. It startled Fourcere but he wasn't about to give ground to this bully. "Ok, find the Russian. But do it quick."

"And Soutier," the director waited while Soutier turned back, "when we finish this, you might want to get yourself a new suit." The blood rose instantly in Soutier's neck and face. It was all he could do to keep himself from going back and slapping the smirk off the little bastard's silly face.

Chapter Sixteen

"Louis, it's Maurice." The policeman's familiar voice came over the phone and faintly echoed off the bare walls of the old bastide.

"Bonjour, mon ami. You have news?"

"Oui, you were right. They are trying to sell the painting themselves. Imagine, the Inspector and the Director of the Museum trying to play this game."   Maurice chuckled. "I knew that the inspector could never do it himself. He's always tried to grab credit from me and other officers, so I thought I would try to help.

As soon as I saw his half-witted assistant in the station, I had an imaginary conversation on the phone. I was discreet but loud enough for Poulenc to overhear me talking of the Russian who had been asking around Provence about art that might be available without too many questions to be asked."

"He shot out of the room like a fox with his tail on fire. Within two hours he was back badgering me with questions. Did I know how to contact the Russian?

Could he really afford to buy expensive art? Was he in Provence now? How did he pay?"

 Louis thought with some sadness that everyone had a Jo in their organization.

"I tell you, Louis, he couldn't get the questions out of his mouth fast enough. Apparently they are in quite a hurry. My guess is they're afraid the American will cause trouble if they are too long in finishing the deal.   I told Poulenc that it was my duty as a police officer to help and that I would try to find a way to contact the Russian. His whole demeanor immediately changed."

"He started telling me how they were going to be rich. And he was laughing at the way he and the inspector had frightened the American family almost out of their wits. The man is such an idiot that I was afraid they wouldn't listen to him. But it seems that with being worried about the American and a bad case of greed, they are forgetting to be careful. One must always be careful, is that not right my friend?"

Louis agreed with a laugh. "And did you find a way to contact the Russian?"

"Mai oui, I told Poulenc that I doubted that the Russian

would risk calling the station but if I could find someone who knew how to contact him, he might be persuaded to phone the Director at the museum. You should have seen him, Louis, you would think he was expecting a call from the President of the République himself."

 As soon as he turned tail and ran back to the Inspector, I called the Russian."

"The Russian," Louis was a little surprised, "You actually called the Russian."

"Well, I made a call and talked to someone about the Russian."

"You are a rascal, my friend," Louis chided Maurice. They both laughed.

Chapter Seventeen

Mama had been right when she had sent Louis back to Aix and not let him give in to his fears. She had laid out her idea on how to make the policeman a part of their plan. She told Louis it would be good to have the law on their side for a change. Louis had had his doubts at first but he now conceded that Mama was quite a wily old woman and that it did no good to argue with her; in fact it was quite smart not to.

Not only had Maurice been a very helpful partner in their unusual business dealings but he had become a friend. More than a friend, almost the brother that Louis had never had. Louis had to admire Maurice's ingenuity with the Russian ploy. He had to laugh too.

Their relationship suffered through some of the same foibles that affected most friendships, even families. They'd blame each other for something silly, argue, and then over a glass of wine or pastis forget what the whole thing had been about. Louis remembered laughing so hard at Maurice on one occasion that he choked and spewed red wine all over a table cloth in their favorite café. Maurice's face had flushed to the color of the wine and had stalked off only to apologize when he had time to think it over.

It began when Maurice had asked Louis to bring an additional piece from the chateau when he came to Aix the following week. Maurice was quick to explain that the need was not his but his mothers. She had had difficulty in seeing well for years but steadfastly refused to see a doctor about eyeglasses. 'Too expensive,' was her argument. She needed her little bit of money for necessities like food and tobacco.

Nevertheless, she kept up a constant stream of complaints about not being able to see. She couldn't see to cook or do housework. She was dependent on others when she would rather do for herself. Her stamina was undaunted. Maurice thought that if he could provide her with a little extra money, she would relent and get the glasses she so badly needed.

Maurice's plan worked perfectly and his mother was fitted with bold new glasses. They were such a hit that she eventually stopped complaining about the terrible cost of a little wire and a couple of slivers of glass.

Problems, however, soon arose for the unlikeliest of reasons. His mother's vision improved too much. Now that she could see everything so much more clearly, she began to see many other things to complain about. The sloppy housekeeping at Maurice's little bungalow, the fact that Maurice's wife had apparently let herself go to ruin in recent years. And of course she regretted that Maurice himself seemed to be looking older. The younger generation didn't care what they looked like anymore.

Maurice had told Louis that several times he had been tempted to grind her new glasses under his heel if he thought it would stop her complaining. Of course when Louis' response was a hearty laugh, it was too much for poor Maurice.

As Louis reminisced about their friendship and waited, he wondered how long it would take for Maurice's little call to the 'Russian' to bear fruit. Louis also wondered how the poor American and his family were holding up. Maurice had found out about their ordeal at the station with Soutier and Poulenc. He felt sorry for them and the more he heard of their misfortunes, the more he wished he could help them out of their predicament.

Chapter Eighteen

The museum Director dialed the Inspector's private line. Soutier finally answered after several rings. Fourcere could hear laughter still ringing in the background. "Oui, Inspector Soutier here."

Fourcere heard a hand clamp over the phone and another round of laughter.

"Inspector," he said loudly and a little impatiently "if I'm interrupting something, perhaps I can call back."

"Ah, Monsieur directeur, it's you," Soutier said. Poulenc was just telling me how he had to be a little rough with DesVaux to get the information we needed."

"And I got the call." Fourcere interrupted. "The Russian can meet with us tomorrow after the museum closes." He knew he had Soutier's complete attention.

"Did you not ask him to come sooner? Is he not now in Aix. It's getting difficult to hold the American?"

It gave Fourcere immense pleasure to say it, "Patience,

Inspector." He tried to make the word 'patience' sound as condescending as possible. "Remember, it was your idea to practically imprison the American. Or was it the idea of that idiot Poulenc?"

Before Soutier could reply with his own venom, Fourcere dropped the bomb, "I suggested a number to the Russian." Fourcere could feel absolute tension crackling down the line. The handset throbbed against his ear.

He told Soutier the amount he had asked of the Russian and heard a quick catch of breath from the other end.

"That's impossible," Soutier thundered, "You'll drive him away, You idiot . ."

"He agreed." Said Fourcere, now in control. Another catch of breath followed by, "Mon Dieu, Director, that's incredible. " After an impossible silence and much heavy breathing, "We're going to be rich."

Fourcere, pleased that he was once again 'The Director' went on, "The only condition is that the painting pass a couple of tests that can be done in a few minutes here in my office. I've looked at the painting ever since the American brought it in. I'm certain that it is absolutely authentic."

The Inspector was suddenly feeling expansive, "great work, Fourcere, I'll take care of the American until tomorrow ."

It rankled Fourcere all over again for Soutier to use his name instead of his title. The pig had no respect for people of position.   The Director could slap back. As sharply as he could, he said, "Be in my office tomorrow at 8:00 P.M." It pleased him that he had made it sound like an order.

Soutier's first impulse was to lash right back at the director, but he held himself. He was going to be rich. Who cared about that now.   "At 8:00 o'clock," he said flatly.

Chapter Nineteen

The Director had been pacing the bare wood floor of his office for a half hour. He couldn't sit down. Every step resounded like a drum beating out his departure. This would be the last time he would have to spend a minute in this dismal room. He had thought much about where he would go to start his new life. It was a very pleasant way to pass the time while he waited.

 Little else had occupied his mind for the past several hours, but then a sharp knock at the door startled him out of his reverie. He looked at the clock above the door, it was a quarter before 8:00. "Entrée," he called. When the door opened Soutier charged as if he were surprising some criminals at their illegal activity. When Fourcere saw that Poulenc followed right behind, he wondered, with malice, why Soutier had to bring that clown.

Both policemen walked about the office as if it were a room in the museum, looking at nothing on the walls, because there was nothing to look at. The director didn't want to talk to them and they didn't want to talk to him. No one wanted to talk to anyone else. It was just the waiting.

At 8:15, with the Russian 15 minutes late, Soutier could contain himself no longer, "Where is the painting?" he asked the Director.

Fourcere was about to open his mouth with a sharp answer, but the phone started to ring and saved him the bother. He grabbed it, pressed it hard to his ear so the two policemen wouldn't be able to hear anything and after a few seconds uttered one word - "Oui."

He turned to Soutier, "He's here." The tension in the room reached detonation point.

A quick rap on the door and it swung open. Fourcere's assistant showed the Russian in. He was carrying a large briefcase that neither Fourcere, Soutier nor Poulenc could take their eyes off. None of them gave a first look at the Russian himself; none of them cared what he looked like.

Without waiting to be offered a chair, the Russian took one right across from Fourcere, hoisted the briefcase to his lap. He folded his hands on top of the briefcase and came immediately to the point burning in everyone's mind, "I vill see zee painting now."

Just like a crude Russian, thought Fourcere, no pleasantries or preliminaries. A similar thought passed through Soutier's mind but he really was quite thankful. Who wanted to waste time exchanging banal pleasantries with a Russian.

Fourcere opened the top drawer of the desk and laid the painting on the broad expanse of the desk top. The Russian reached for it, unrolled it and studied it for only a few seconds.   Soutier had watched as the Russian had lifted the briefcase to his lap and thought how heavy it must be. Just how heavy was that much money?

The Russian rummaged through a smaller bag that looked like it might contain testing tools or equipment but stopped and pulled a cell phone from his pocket. "I must call my colleague, for I have forgotten something I must need to conduct zee test. Without waiting for any kind of agreement from Soutier or the Director, he dialed a number and in a couple of rings barked a few sharp orders in what Soutier and Fourcere assumed to be Russian, although neither had ever heard anyone speak a word of Russian before that moment.

The longer the Russian looked at the painting, Soutier and Fourcere grew more breathless. Their anticipation was at a fever pitch. Wealth was moments away. How could one wait?

"So, zee American was trying to steal zee painting." The Russian tried to break the tension while they waited.

"No, monsieur," Poulenc could not stand the quiet either, "he was just trying to turn it in to somebody, just get rid of it. I had to give him a good scare to make sure he wouldn't talk about it before we were ready." Both Soutier and Fourcere would have liked to gag him but it didn't matter much now. It was all but over and he could brag all he wanted. They'd both soon be out of France and within a week the fool would implicate himself and he could be the goat for all of them. Fourcere thought it would be a good ending all round.

A knock on the door broke the spell. The Russian put the briefcase back on the floor, rose from his chair and started for the door, "that vill be my colleague now." When he opened the door he pulled it fully open. Fourcere, Soutier, and Poulenc had momentarily pried their attention from the briefcase that the Russian had placed on the floor and looked with confusion at the two hard faces staring back at them. They had the look of men who wouldn't welcome argument. They were quickly into the room and looked to the Russian for orders.

The Russian turn back to Soutier and Fourcere and announced, "Good evening Monsieurs, let me introduce myself, I am agent Luc DuBois of Interpol, and these gentlemen are my colleagues." DuBois gave them a few seconds for his statement to sink in. "You gentlemen are under arrest for conspiring to steal a French national treasure - among other charges. Soutier and Fourcere suddenly tottered on weak knees and sank to their seats. Poulenc fell to the floor in a dead faint, his head making a drum like sound as it bounced on the bare planks.

DuBois took Poulenc's handcuffs, held them out to his colleagues and nodded toward Soutier and Fourcere. "Cuff them together and to that pipe by the wall." He looked at Poulenc crumpled up on the floor, "and get this man some medical attention and take him out for questioning."

"I would tell you gentlemen not to move, but that probably isn't necessary." DuBois smiled smugly. "I'll be back for you after I have taken care of this one." He pointed at Poulenc and then picked up the painting and rolling it up and returned it to its tube. A whimper escaped Fourcere's throat and a groan from Soutier's as they watched their fortune disappear into the

162

cardboard tube like some animal wriggling free of the hunter's grasp and escaping back into its burrow.

"Think carefully about what you have done." DuBois sternly advised, "But you will have plenty of time for that, won't you - perhaps even as cellmates. He took the tube and followed the other agents as they carried Poulenc out and gave the door a thunderous slam.

Both Soutier and Fourcere felt like screaming, hoping that being in a cell together was not to be a part of their punishment. With no other way to express his frustration, Soutier gave a sharp jerk on the handcuffs and at least had the satisfaction of hearing a bark of pain from Fourcere.

After the better part of an hour spent bickering, blaming and incriminating each other, they finally heard footfalls on the other side of the door announcing the return of DuBois. A knock on the door brought the question to both of their minds as to why DuBois would knock. Unhappily realizing that to say "Go away" probably wouldn't work, Fourcere finally mumbled a grudging 'entrée'. When the door swung open, Soutier and Fourcere were thoroughly bewildered by the faces now glaring at them.

"Who are you," cried Fourcere. "Where's DuBois?"

"Who's DuBois, answered Maurice Desvaux.

"He's the Russian," said Soutier who stopped in mid sentence, realizing that something was very wrong. He was also beginning to realize the oddity of a Russian named DuBois. He needed answers, "And what are you doing here, Desvaux?"

"Bon Soir to you Inspector. I think you already know monsieur Baker and let me introduce Colonel Andre Puylaurent of the French Police Nationale."

Soutier quickly added up the situation and came up with no answers, at least none that seemed to be in his favor. With Poulenc already taken away and not there to defend himself, he just as quickly saw his chance to recover and put the blame for everything on Poulenc.

"Desvaux," Soutier tried to sound commanding, "get these cuffs off us."

He tried to muster a look of personal relief at seeing Baker in good health "Monsieur Baker, I sincerely hope that you and your family are OK. I hope that devil Poulenc didn't frighten your poor wife and daughter too

164

much. I didn't know that Poulenc and his thugs had dragged you all about Aix in that terrible van. I'm sorry, but we had to play along like that to trap Poulenc and thanks to you, we have. He finally showed his hand tonight and it looks like he's involved with some Russian criminal pretending to be from Interpol. They have stolen the painting that you, Monsieur Baker, so graciously returned to this museum."

"That's a great story, Soutier," Colonel Puylaurent cut him short, "But Monsieur Baker will testify as to your involvement and your van driver is on his way to Marseille with two of my colleagues. As far as DuBois, or whoever he is, we shall catch him too. So you and Monsieur Fourcere can get used to the cuffs."

"I had no part in this awful thing," cried Fourcere. "I had no idea what Soutier and Poulent had planned. I was simply trying to see that such a wonderful painting was recovered for France."

Being bested by Desvaux, betrayed by Poulenc, and blamed for everything by Fourcere , it was too much for Soutier. His confession began as a trickle and soon the flood engulfed himself, Fourcere, Poulenc and several other accomplices in their scheme to steal the Cezanne and even their thefts from the museum.

Puylaurent, Desvaux, and Baker realized they'd caught two of the crooks but had missed one and lost the painting in the process.

"I've never heard of an agent DuBois at Interpol", Puylaurent said, "I have to assume that he is an accomplice of Poulenc's."

"Colonel, while you deal with these two, I must make a call," said Maurice. "Monsieur Baker, would you come with me please?"

Maurice and Sam hurried across the street to the café to find a phone.

Chapter Twenty

Louis waited at the bastide for the outcome of the bust at the museum. That was as close as he wanted to be to such an affair. He no longer had any expectation of getting the painting back but simply wanted to see how the whole thing played out. Watching was how one learned. He was beginning to realize where he had made some crucial errors – errors that he would not make again.

His cell phone rang. "Louis, this is Maurice. I'm afraid I have bad news. That little devil Poulenc has fooled us all. He and his accomplice have double-crossed Soutier and Fourcere and have stolen the painting for themselves. By the time Colonel Puylaurent and I could find Monsieur Baker and his family and then rush here, they'd gone and left Soutier and Fourcere to take the punishment. Looks as if we have come up empty again." Maurice cupped his hand over the phone and lowered his voice. "Monsieur Baker is especially disappointed. I think he had wanted a few words alone with Poulenc.

"Ah," said Louis,

"Ah, what? replied Maurice.

"Now it makes sense."

"What makes sense?" Maurice was straining to follow Louis' thinking.

"Why Poulenc left the museum without Soutier and Fourcere *and* before you , Monsieur Baker and the Colonel could arrive. He somehow found out about your plans and decided to strike first."

"How do you know this already?" Maurice's amazement at Louis was growing along with his befuddlement at the situation.

"Paulo was there across the street, watching. As soon as he saw the Russian – or whoever he is – come in after hours, he called me. And when they left with Poulenc before you could get there, I had Paulo follow them."

"Where are they now?" Maurice asked hopefully.

"They drove straight to an apartment building on Boulevard du clos Gabriel. It's out past the autoroute. Paulo said Poulenc's name is on a mailbox there."

"So Poulenc went home. . . probably to pack," said Maurice. "Sounds like he's getting out."

"Wouldn't you?" chuckled Louis.

"I must see the Colonel immediately," said Maurice.

Louis could hear two pairs of footfalls starting for the door even as the line was going dead.

Chapter Twenty-One

"We can't stay here too long," Poulenc told the Russian, who was actually his cousin Max. "Soutier is an idiot but that Desvaux is one to watch out for. It won't take him long to put everything together and come looking. Let me pack a few things and we'll be out of here."

"After we turn this painting into cash, you can take up acting?" said Max. "that little faint and the noise you made as you hit the floor. Magnifique!"

"And you, cousin, you make a great Russian. The accent, incroyable!" Poulenc laughed through yellow teeth. "As soon as you had called the director, he was on the phone to Soutier bragging about the price you were going to pay for the painting. Soutier was actually salivating on the phone. I'd love to see his face when he finally figures out what has happened. Always thinks he's smarter than everyone else. Never thought that his assistant was anything but a fool." Poulenc was getting rid of years of frustrations. "He got what he deserves,"

"And that museum man," added Max, "they'll be at each other's throats like two sailors in a Marseille bar.

Those two wanted to find the Russian so badly to buy this." Max held up the tube, "They would have believed our old uncle was the Russian."

"Who were the two brutes you brought with you?" asked Poulenc.

"Those two," Max laughed, "just a couple of friends who owed me a few Euros. Now we're even. And that's why I was late. Those two have no sense of timing.

"You had me worried," said Poulenc, "so we've got to hurry. I called the station. They said that Desvaux and some Colonel from Police Nationale came and took the Bakers away."

Poulenc stuffed more clothes in a grungy duffle. "When we sell this," he took the painting from Max and put it in on top of his clothes, "We'll throw this junk away and dress like the riche on the Cote D'Azur and.."

A thunderous crash landed against the apartment door. Before Poulenc and Max could do more than look startled, another thud landed. Wood splintered around the door lock and flew through the room like shrapnel; the door itself almost ripping off its hinges.

171

Puylaurent, Desvaux and Baker burst into the room with the momentum of battering rams. Puylaurent and Desvaux quickly cuffed Max who looked like the one that might offer some trouble and Sam backed Poulenc into a corner. Poulenc swallowed hard and lowered his hand to his weapon.

"Unless you want to eat that," Sam growled and shoved Poulenc hard in the chest, "You'd better put those hands in the air."

Poulenc turned pale and reached for the ceiling. Sam was tempted to take just a little revenge for what Poulenc had put him and his family through, but knew that wasn't his style. He clenched his huge fists and let Poulenc worry for several seconds about what he was going to do. Sam did wonder, though, if punching a prison-bound policeman in the nose would be considered bad form by the French.

Poulenc was about to plead for mercy when Sam grabbed him by the collar and shoved him toward the door.

Chapter Twenty-Two

Louis had chosen a table by the window in the little Viet Namese café in Aix where Maurice DesVaux, the policeman, and he had first sparred over lunch so many months before. Where, for all the weeks since, they had steadily forged an improbable but genuine friendship and continued their mutual business arrangement and campaign for justice. He wanted to be by the window so he could see when Maurice was approaching the restaurant. Maurice had called after the finale of events in Aix.

He had regaled Louis with the juicy story of the downfall of Soutier and the crooked museum director. And Poulenc, the disgusting little fool, squealed like a sanglier caught in the thistles. He told everything he knew about his boss and the museum director.   There was no shutting him up. And then the even better story of the American and his family and how they were now heroes of the République.

 Even he, Maurice, would receive a special commendation for his part in recovering a French national treasure

But then his countenance had audibly fallen. Louis could almost see his expression change over the phone wire. Maurice regretted that Louis was the only one to emerge from the affair with no benefit. He would like to sit with his friend and buy him a pastis at the least; lunch, if Louis still had any appetite.

But first, he would like to bring along the Baker family. They were still in Aix and very much wanted to meet Louis, and Maurice knew that Louis wanted to apologize for dragging them into this mess and destroying their vacation.

How could he answer but to say 'yes.' Louis wondered if the American was still angry and would want to take revenge for his cracked head. Louis felt quite sure that Baker knew who was responsible for that and the pilfering of his wallet in Aix. And who could tell what retribution the American would want to exact for the terror to his wife and daughter. Louis figured that he could somehow be considered responsible for that too.

There was no doubt in Louis' mind that there would be some unpleasantness but he could not live with himself without at least trying to make an apology. Perhaps the American's anger had cooled over the last three of four days. He hoped so.

174

Louis had, in fact, already fortified himself with a large glass of pastis when he saw Maurice coming along the street in front of the restaurant. The American family walked with him. They seemed to be talking in a friendly manner but it was hard for Louis to imagine what mood the big American might be in. Ironically, Louis thought, he should be a happy man. He had a pretty wife and daughter, a nice family. That was important.

Louis stood as they entered the restaurant and approached the table. Louis wore a hesitant smile, hoping it might be contagious. Maurice introduced the Bakers. Kisses for the women and a handshake with monsieur Baker.

Louis always thought that a good firm handshake was an indication of strong character. He was already beginning to like this American. Louis had taken the precaution of ordering a large carafe of both the local white and rose wines. He didn't want to have a void of quiet hanging over the table as they began their rendezvous. He firmly believed in the good camaraderie generated by good wine.

Louis poured wine all around and bravely suggested a toast to everyone's health and happiness. He was encouraged by the fact that the Bakers did not object and agreeably clinked glasses.

This seemed an opportune time to offer up his apology. Louis had been thinking about what he should say and how he could best say it. He wanted to say he was sorry but before he could get very far, Diane held up a hand. Louis stopped and swallowed hard, wary of what might be coming.

"You needn't worry monsieur Jaubert," Diane said, "And you don't need to apologize. I should be grateful to you."

Louis was thinking there was no end to the strangeness of the Americans and the peculiar way they thought. Perhaps she hadn't understood what he was trying to say. He looked around the table for a clue.

Maurice and Sam and the Baker's daughter were all beginning to break into a big grin as Diane continued, "No, really, I must thank you for making this the best vacation we've ever had."

Louis was now certain that the Baker woman was a bit crazy. To thank him, it was *incroyable.*

She explained, "My husband had wanted to go with his

friends on an adventure vacation." She raised her eyebrows at Louis as if asking him to confirm that he understood. He nodded and she continued, "I was afraid that he wasn't enjoying our trip very much and that I would never get him back to France again." She looked toward Sam, "I was afraid I had been too insistent on his coming to France and that he was bored and secretly wishing he was with his buddies down in that old canyon. No adventure here, you know."

Diane brightened, "Now, he's had an authentic Cezanne worth a fortune dropped in his lap, he's been mugged in one hotel room, robbed in another, practically tortured and bullied by the police only to be rescued by Officer DesVaux and agents of Le Police Nationale. Then he gets to pretend he's on a SWAT team and even had a chance to give that Poulenc a good thumping. And now he's been given an award by the République Francaise. He's been made un Chevalier de l'Ordre des Arts et des Lettres de France for helping to recover a French national treasure. And," she hesitated for emphasis, "He has a medal to show for it. He's an authentic knight of the République Francais."

Louis was astonished, "Mai non!"

"She's right", Sam Said, "I'm not sure we'd have

survived much more 'adventure' but now a trip to someplace like the Grand canyon would be boring in comparison." Sam looked at Diane and Beth and back at Louis, "We're already planning to come back next year." Sam's grin broadened until all his teeth showed, "And why not, I am, after all, a knight of the République."

All the other patrons of the little café saw the wonderful joie de vie at the table by the window and held up their glasses in salute.

Chapter Twenty-Three

After the Bakers left to continue their much delayed tour of Aix, Louis and Maurice sat quietly and drank their wine. Maurice was unsure of what to say, of how to buoy up his friend. He could see the earlier cheer melting away. He looked at Louis with pity, "My friend you look so troubled. I am so sorry that our plans have ended this badly." He tried to brighten the situation, "At least the République gained something from it all. Now we will have our friend, Cezanne, back in Provence."

Maurice went on as he moved his chair closer to Louis. This was nothing for other curious ears to hear. He leaned in, "What would we have done with all that money anyway, eh"? He tried to sound jovial, but his bonhomie faded in the face of Louis' gloom.

"Mon Dieu, listen to me. What am I saying? I could have used some of it for Mama's doctors now that she has become so ill." His look reflected that on Louis' face. "The terrible part is, I too, had to endure a conversation with that abominable Russian. He says that the French are

179

too sentimental and let it get in the way of business.

Can you believe that? He called me - a policeman - sentimental. He even had the bad manners to rub it in. Said he not only would have paid a top price for the Cezanne but as soon as things are cleared up in Marseille, he would be looking to buy much more art for another 'collector'.

Louis said nothing, resignedly staring at his glass as he moved it around in little circles on the table.

Maurice felt a need to fill the silence. "Not only have we lost the painting, but with the old madam gone, the Chateau - as you know — will probably be confiscated for taxes by the government. We shall no longer have reason to meet and enjoy a lunch together and share the spoils of the old Nazi." Maurice stopped and smacked the heel of his hand against his forehead, "Listen to me, what am I saying? Of course we'll meet, we're friends but I'm afraid that our campaign of justice, sadly, has run its course."   He smiled wanly and then looked at Louis with unhappy and sympathetic eyes, "my friend, you say nothing. You look so melancholy.   What can I say to console you? What can I do?" Maurice now felt as distraught as Louis looked.

180

"I thank you for your concern my friend," Louis said with a choke in his voice, "but you must not worry too much about me." He lowered his head and covered his face with his big hands, the words hanging between them like brittle and shattered dreams. The defeated expression on Louis' face stabbed Maurice like a stiletto to the heart. Maurice tried to say something but felt helpless, unable to offer any comfort to his friend.

The truth was, Louis was having a very hard time fighting to keep the downcast, hangdog look on his face and when he stole a look through parted fingers he was surprised at the effect his act was having on his friend. Enough, he thought, he had to confess. Now!

Louis put his hands back on the table and looked up at Maurice. "Do you remember when I told you that the old Nazi had stolen the Cezanne from his boss?" He waited for full dramatic effect, picked up his glass and slowly drained it for good measure. "I may have forgotten to tell you the whole story."

Maurice worried that his friend was leading up to more bad news. He should have gotten there earlier, he chided himself. Louis had taken too much comfort from the bottle when what he had needed was human friendship, his friendship. Now all that Maurice could do was to humor him, "What is it that you have forgotten, my friend?" He laid a tender hand on Louis' shoulder.

A hundred watt smile was breaking out on Louis' face in spite of his best efforts to contain it. "Did I ever say anything about the other paintings?" He quickly amended "*our* other paintings?"

 Maurice was taken aback and a bit slow in changing directions, "What is it you are talking about?" While he waited for Louis' answer, his mind slowly began knitting together bits of information that Louis had dropped in conversation during those many market day lunches in Aix. As it started to add up, a thin smile began to tug at the corners his dark, well trimmed moustache. " Are you telling me that . .uh . .uh. .there's more paintings?"

Louis beamed at his friend and nodded. Maurice gently jabbed Louis in the chest with a finger, "You old villain, you sit there laughing inside while I worry about you. Maybe that awful Russian is right – I am too sentimental"

As they clinked glasses, Maurice's face took on a more

serious expression, "Does this mean we will continue our crusade for justice?"

"Bien sur, mon ami, of course, my friend, if not us, then who?"

Between his own commendation and the American receiving a knighthood, Maurice still felt that Louis had been left on the short end of things. "Perhaps now you will think of doing a little something for yourself, non?"

Louis pushed out his lips, narrowed his eyes and gave the impression of giving much consideration to his answer,

"I think I just might buy the old bastide after all," he finally said with a wry smile. And then with a wink, added "But first . . . . . there's a matter of a few Croissants."

THE END

Thanks for Reading!

Made in the USA
Lexington, KY
11 March 2014